JN272158

英⇔和 心理学用語集

心理学用語研究会 編

培風館

本書の無断複写は，著作権法上での例外を除き，禁じられています．
本書を複写される場合は，その都度当社の許諾を得てください．

まえがき

　本書は，心理学の幅広い分野にわたる用語（約 2700 語）と，人名（238 名）を収録した英和・和英対訳集です。初学者から大学院入試，公務員試験対策など，いろいろな用途に対応できるよう，多くの用語を集める一方で，特に初歩的な用語（約 300 語）を**太字**で示し，人名には関連するキーワードを付すといった工夫をしています。心理学を専攻する大学生には，使い込んで「必携の一冊」だと実感してもらいたいと思います。

　近年，社会のグローバル化の流れに伴い，大学教育においても英語での専門授業や英語テキストを使用しての授業が望まれています。心理学も例外ではありません。日本語だけにとどまっていては，せっかく学んだ心理学の専門知識も外国人と英語で話すときには十分に活かすことができません。たとえば，臨床心理学の授業で「自閉症」についてしっかり学んでいたとしても "autism" という英語を知らなければ，臨床活動はおろか日常会話でも困ります。外国人の友人から "My child has autism" と話しかけられた際，"autism" って何のことだろう，とぽかんとした顔をしていたら，「この人ホントに心理学を大学で勉強したの？」と思われてしまうでしょう。

　したがって専門用語は日本語だけでなく英語でも憶える必要があります。しかし，上記の「自閉症」と "autism" のように，対応する訳語が普通の和英／英和辞典にも掲載されている場合はまれです。たとえば，ある英和辞典には "discrimination" の第一義として「差別」があり，第二義として「識別」が掲載されています。しかし，実験心理学の論文では多くの場合，この語は刺激間の区別を意味しており，「弁別」と訳すことになっています。それを知らなければ，"discrimination between A and B"

i

を「AとBの差別」と訳して意味が分からなくなったり,「AとBの識別」と訳して専門家から失笑をかったりします（後者の場合，意味的には問題がないのですが，専門用語に無知で恥をかくということです）。

「誤訳」を避け，最初から適切な訳をするためには心理学辞典を手元に用意しておく必要があります。ところが，現在，手ごろなサイズの心理学辞典には新しい用語が掲載されておらず，新しい用語も網羅した心理学辞典は大きくて携帯に不便です。このため，心理学の英文講読に際して，学生に薦められる対訳集が欲しいとわれわれは考えました。そこで，授業教材で扱う用語にはじまり，心理学領域すべてをカバーできるように十年程前から用語の選定などを行い，数年前の私家版を経てようやく本書の公刊に至りました。本書と似たタイプの用語集は，すでに2〜3点が出版されておりますが，本書は基礎系心理学の用語を重視して用語選定を行った点に違いがあります。

最後に，本書が皆さんのお手元に届けられるのも，培風館のご協力を得てのことです。取締役社長 山本 格氏並びに編集部の近藤妙子氏に心から感謝申し上げます。

2014年3月

　　　　　　　　　　　執筆者を代表して
　　　　　　　　　　　　鈴木 まや・中島 定彦

凡　例

　本書は，心理学関連領域の用語の英和・和英対訳を収録した〈用語集〉と，研究者名を収録した〈人名集〉から構成される。

＜用　語　集＞
1. 英語のアルファベット順に配列した「英→和」と，日本語の50音順に配列した「和→英」の2つに分けている。
2. 心理学領域での初歩的な用語（約300語）は，**太字**で表記した。
3. 英語表記において，同義語は；（セミコロン），略称は原綴りの後に，（カンマ）を付けて表記した。
4. 不規則に変化する単数・複数形は，英語の後ろに（単数：　）等として併記した。
5. 語句の補足的な説明等には《　》を付した。
6. 省略可能な部分には（　）を付した。
7. 言い換え可能な部分には〔　〕を付した。
8. 略語は⇨で，原綴りを参照するようにした。

＜人　名　集＞
1. 欧文表記順「英→和」と，カタカナ表記の50音順「和→英」に配列した2つに分けている。
2. 公開されている生誕年を表記した。
3. 人名表記の下に，人物にまつわるキーワードを表記した。
4. キーワード中に，『　』に入れて示したものは主要著書である。

用語集

A

☐ ABAB design	ABAB計画法
☐ abdominal breathing	腹式呼吸
☐ **abnormal**	**異常**
☐ abnormal behavior	異常行動
☐ absent-mindedness	放心(状態)
☐ absolute threshold	絶対閾
☐ **abstract**	**要約,抽象(的)**
☐ abstraction	抽象化
☐ **abuse**	**虐待**
☐ acceptance	受容
☐ accessibility	接近可能性
☐ accommodation	調節,(水晶体の)調整作用
☐ accountability	説明責任
☐ achievement motive	達成動機
☐ acquisition	習得,獲得
☐ acrophase	頂点位相
☐ act psychology	作用心理学
☐ action potential	活動電位
☐ activated sleep	賦活睡眠
☐ active attention	能動的注意
☐ active listening	積極的傾聴
☐ **activity**	**活動,活動性**
☐ activity of daily living, ADL	日常生活動作
☐ actor-observer bias	行為者-観察者バイアス
☐ acute stress disorder	急性ストレス障害
☐ **adaptation**	**順応,適応**
☐ adaptive behavior	適応行動
☐ addiction	嗜癖
☐ additive factor method	加算要因法
☐ ADHD	⇨ attention deficit/hyperactivity disorder
☐ adjective check list, ACL	形容詞チェックリスト

☐ adjustment heuristic	調整ヒューリスティック
☐ **adolescence**	**青年期**
☐ adolescent growth spurt	青年期発達加速
☐ adrenaline	アドレナリン
☐ **adulthood**	**成人期**
☐ **affect**	**感情, 情動**
☐ affective meaning	情緒的意味
☐ affective neuroscience	情動神経科学
☐ afferent nerve	求心性神経
☐ affiliation	所属機関
☐ affiliation motive	親和動機
☐ affiliative conflict	親和葛藤
☐ affordance	アフォーダンス
☐ after effect	残効
☐ after image	残像
☐ agape	アガペー, 愛《キリスト教的な》
☐ **aggression**	**攻撃性**
☐ aggressive behavior	攻撃行動
☐ aging	エイジング, 加齢
☐ agnosia	失認
☐ agonist	作用薬
☐ agoraphobia	広場恐怖(症)
☐ agrammatism	失文法
☐ agreeableness	調和性
☐ aha experience	アハ体験, ハハァ経験
☐ alcoholism	アルコール中毒(症)〔依存(症)〕
☐ alexithymia	アレキシサイミア, 失感情症
☐ algorithm	アルゴリズム, 算法
☐ aloneness	孤独感
☐ alternative hypothesis	対立仮説
☐ altruism	愛他性, 利他性
☐ altruistic behavior	愛他行動
☐ Alzheimer's disease	アルツハイマー病

☐ ambivalence	アンビバレンス,両価性,両義性	
☐ American Psychiatric Association, APA	アメリカ精神医学会	
☐ American Psychological Association, APA	アメリカ心理学会	
☐ amnesia	健忘(症),記憶の障害	
☐ amphetamine	アンフェタミン	
☐ amplitude	振幅	
☐ amusia	失音楽症	
☐ amygdala	扁桃体	
☐ anal stage	肛門期	
☐ analogical representation	アナログ表象	
☐ analogy	類推	
☐ analysis of covariance, ANCOVA	共分散分析	
☐ **analysis of variance, ANOVA**	**分散分析**	
☐ analytic thought	分析的思考	
☐ anchoring effect	係留効果	
☐ androgyny	両性性,両性具有	
☐ **anger**	**怒り**	
☐ anger control	怒りの制御	
☐ anger in	怒りの抑制	
☐ anger out	怒りの表出	
☐ anhedonia	快楽喪失	
☐ animism	アニミズム	
☐ anomic aphasia	失名辞失語症,失名詞症	
☐ anonymity	匿名性,無名性	
☐ anorexia nervosa	神経性無食欲症	
☐ ANOVA	⇨ analysis of variance	
☐ antagonist	拮抗薬,敵対者	
☐ antecedent	先行刺激,前件	
☐ anterograde amnesia	前向性健忘	
☐ anthropology	人類学	
☐ anticipatory response	予期的反応	

☐ antidepressant	抗うつ薬
☐ antisocial behavior	反社会的行動
☐ antisocial personality	反社会性パーソナリティ
☐ antisocial personality disorder	反社会性パーソナリティ障害
☐ **anxiety**	**不安**
☐ anxiety disorder	不安症〔障害〕
☐ anxiety hierarchy	不安の階層
☐ APA	⇨ American Psychiatric Association
☐ APA	⇨ American Psychological Association
☐ apathy	アパシー, 無感動
☐ aphasia	失語症
☐ apparent movement	仮現運動, 仮視運動
☐ apperception	統覚
☐ appetitive conditioning	食餌性条件づけ
☐ **applied behavior analysis**	**応用行動分析**
☐ applied psychology	応用心理学
☐ **approach**	**接近**
☐ approach-approach conflict	接近-接近葛藤
☐ approach-avoidance conflict	接近-回避葛藤
☐ approach learning	有益刺激への接近学習
☐ approval	承認
☐ aptitude	適性
☐ arbitrary	恣意性
☐ archetype	元型, アーキタイプ
☐ archicortex	原皮質
☐ **arousal**	**覚醒, 喚起**
☐ arousal level	覚醒水準
☐ arousal theory	覚醒理論
☐ art therapy	芸術療法
☐ artificial intelligence	人工知能
☐ ascending series〔trial〕	上昇系列〔試行〕

用語(英→和) am〜as

☐ assertion	自己主張	
☐ assertion training	自己主張訓練, アサーション・トレーニング	
☐ **assessment**	**査定, 評価, アセスメント**	
☐ assimilation	同化	
☐ **association**	**連合, アソシエーション**	
☐ association area	連合野	
☐ associationism	連合主義	
☐ associationist psychology	連合主義心理学	
☐ associative learning	連合学習	
☐ associative strength	連合強度	
☐ **attachment**	**愛着**	
☐ **attention**	**注意**	
☐ attention deficit/hyperactivity disorder, ADHD	注意欠如・多動症〔障害〕	
☐ attention theory	注意説	
☐ attentional trace	注意痕跡説	
☐ **attitude**	**態度**	
☐ attributable risk	寄与リスク	
☐ **attribution**	**帰属**	
☐ attribution process	帰属過程	
☐ attribution theory	帰属理論	
☐ attributional style	帰属様式	
☐ atypical antipsychotics	非定型抗精神病薬	
☐ **audition**	**聴覚**	
☐ auditory cue	聴覚的手がかり	
☐ auditory system	聴覚系	
☐ authenticity	本来感, 自分らしさ	
☐ author	著者	
☐ authoritarian personality	権威主義的パーソナリティ	
☐ authority	権威	
☐ **autism**	**自閉症**	
☐ autism spectrum disorder, ASD	自閉スペクトラム症	

☐ autistic disorder	自閉性障害
☐ autobiographical memory	自伝的記憶
☐ autogenic training	自律訓練法
☐ autokinetic	自動運動
☐ automatic process	自動的処理〔過程〕
☐ automaticity	自動性
☐ **autonomic nervous system, ANS**	**自律神経系**
☐ autonomic response	自律反応
☐ autonomic thoughts	自動思考
☐ autonomy	自律性
☐ autoshaping	自動形成, オートシェイピング
☐ auxiliary hypothesis	補助仮説
☐ availability	利用可能性
☐ availability heuristic	利用可能性ヒューリスティック
☐ averaged EP, AEP	加算誘発電位
☐ aversion therapy	嫌悪療法
☐ aversive conditioning	嫌悪条件づけ
☐ **avoidance**	**回避**
☐ avoidance-avoidance conflict	回避 − 回避葛藤
☐ avoidance learning	回避学習
☐ **awareness**	**意識性**, 気づき
☐ axon	軸索

B

☐ babbling	喃語
☐ Babinski reflex	バビンスキー反射
☐ back projections	逆行性投射
☐ back propagation	バック・プロパゲーション
☐ background EEG	背景脳波
☐ backward conditioning	逆行条件づけ
☐ backward masking	逆行性マスキング

☐	balance	均衡状態，バランス
☐	balance theory of attitude	態度のバランス理論
☐	bargaining	取り引き
☐	base rate fallacy	基準比率の誤り
☐	baseline	ベースライン
☐	basic level	基礎水準
☐	basic motive	基本的動機
☐	basilar membrane	基底膜
☐	basking in reflected glory	栄光浴
☐	Baumtest	バウムテスト，樹木画テスト
☐	Bayesian statistics	ベイズ統計学
☐	beats per minute, bpm	分時拍動数
☐	Beck Depression Inventory, BDI	ベック抑うつ尺度
☐	**behavior**	**行動**
☐	**behavior analysis**	**行動分析**
☐	behavior assessment	行動アセスメント
☐	behavior disorder	行動障害
☐	behavior genetics	行動遺伝学
☐	**behavior modification**	**行動変容**，行動修正
☐	behavior rehearsal	行動リハーサル
☐	**behavior therapy**	**行動療法**
☐	behavioral assessment	行動評価
☐	behavioral ecology	行動生態学
☐	behavioral economics	行動経済学
☐	behavioral genetics	行動遺伝学
☐	behavioral measure	行動測度
☐	behavioral medicine	行動医学
☐	behavioral observation	行動観察
☐	behavioral risk factors	行動リスク要因
☐	behavioral science	行動科学
☐	behavioral therapy	行動療法
☐	**behaviorism**	**行動主義**

☐ behaviorist	行動主義者	
☐ belief	信念	
☐ belongingness	所属性	
☐ benzodiazepines	ベンゾジアゼピン	
☐ **between-subject(s) design**	**被験者間計画**	
☐ between-subject(s) factor	被験者間要因	
☐ **bias**	**バイアス，偏り**	
☐ biased sample	偏りのある標本	
☐ Big Five	ビッグ・ファイブ，(性格の)主要5因子	
☐ bilateral transfer	両側性転移	
☐ binding problem	結合(の)問題，結びつけ問題	
☐ binocular disparity; binocular parallax	両眼視差	
☐ binominal distribution	二項分布	
☐ **biofeedback, BF**	**バイオフィードバック**	
☐ biological clock	生物時計	
☐ biological constraints on learning	学習の生物的制約	
☐ biological motion	バイオロジカルモーション	
☐ biological psychology	生物心理学	
☐ biological rhythm	生物〔生体〕リズム	
☐ biomedical model	生物医学モデル	
☐ biopsychosocial model	生物心理社会モデル	
☐ bipolar disorder	双極性障害	
☐ blind technique (test)	盲検法，ブラインドテスト	
☐ **blink**	**瞬目，まばたき**	
☐ blink reflex	瞬目反射	
☐ Bloch's law	ブロックの法則	
☐ blocking	ブロッキング，阻止	
☐ blood flow	血流	
☐ blood pressure, BP	血圧	
☐ blood volume	血量	
☐ body image	身体的自己，身体像	

☐ body temperature	体温
☐ borderline personality disorder	境界性パーソナリティ障害
☐ **bottom-up processing**	**ボトムアップ処理**,上昇型処理
☐ bpm	⇨ beats per minute
☐ **brain**	**脳**
☐ brain imaging	脳画像法
☐ brain stem	脳幹
☐ brain stem response, BSR	脳幹反応
☐ brain wave	脳波
☐ brainstem potential	脳幹電位
☐ brainstem reticular formation	脳幹網様体
☐ bridging inference	橋渡しの推論
☐ brief psychotherapy	短期心理療法
☐ brief therapy	短期療法,ブリーフセラピー
☐ brightness	明るさ
☐ Broca's aphasia	ブローカ失語症
☐ Broca's area	ブローカ野《運動性言語中枢》
☐ bulimia nervosa	神経性過食症
☐ burnout	燃え尽き
☐ buttered child syndrome	被虐待児症候群
☐ bystander effect	傍観者効果

C

☐ cannabis	大麻
☐ **Cannon-Bard theory**	**キャノン=バード説**
☐ carryover effect	キャリーオーバー効果,残留効果
☐ case control study	症例コントロール研究
☐ case formulation	ケース構築,ケースフォーミュレーション
☐ case history	事例史
☐ **case study**	**事例研究**
☐ catecholamine	カテコールアミン

☐ categorization	カテゴリー化	
☐ category	カテゴリー	
☐ catharsis	カタルシス，浄化	
☐ cathartic method	カタルシス法	
☐ causal attribution	原因帰属	
☐ **causal relationship**; causality	**因果関係**	
☐ causality heuristic	因果性ヒューリスティック	
☐ ceiling effect	天井効果	
☐ cell assembly	細胞集成体	
☐ central motive state	中枢の動機状態	
☐ **central nervous system, CNS**	**中枢神経系**	
☐ central route	中心経路	
☐ central tendency	中心化傾向	
☐ centrifugal	遠心的	
☐ centripetal	求心的	
☐ cerebellum	小脳	
☐ **cerebral cortex**	**大脳皮質**	
☐ cerebral evoked potential; cerebral EP	大脳誘発電位	
☐ cerebral hemisphere	大脳半球	
☐ cerebral hemorrhage	脳出血	
☐ cerebral infarction	脳梗塞	
☐ cerebral vascular accident	脳血管障害	
☐ cerebrum	大脳	
☐ chain reflex	連鎖反射	
☐ challenge	挑戦	
☐ **character**	**性格**	
☐ characteristic feature	特徴的特性	
☐ chemistry	化学	
☐ chest breathing	胸式呼吸	
☐ **chi square test**	**カイ二乗検定**	
☐ child abuse	児童虐待	
☐ **childhood**	**児童期，幼児期**	

☐ childhood amnesia	幼児期健忘
☐ choice reaction time, CRT	選択反応時間
☐ chroma	彩度
☐ chromosome	染色体
☐ chronic	慢性の
☐ chronological age, CA	生活年齢
☐ chunk	チャンク
☐ chunking	チャンキング
☐ circadian rhythm	概日リズム，サーカディアン・リズム
☐ **classical conditioning**	**古典的条件づけ**
☐ **client**	**来談者，クライアント**
☐ **client centered therapy**	**来談者中心療法，クライエント中心療法**
☐ clinical psychologist	臨床心理学者，臨床心理士
☐ **clinical psychology**	**臨床心理学**
☐ closed-ended question	単一回答式質問
☐ closure	閉合
☐ cluster analysis	クラスター分析
☐ CMI	⇨ Cornell Medical Index
☐ CNS	⇨ central nervous system
☐ coacting group	共行動集団
☐ coaction	共行動
☐ cochlea	蝸牛
☐ cocktail party effect	カクテルパーティ効果
☐ coding	符号化
☐ coefficient alpha	アルファ〔α〕係数
☐ coefficient of concordance	一致係数
☐ coercive power	強制勢力
☐ **cognition**	**認知**
☐ cognitive appraisal	認知の評価
☐ cognitive approach	認知的アプローチ
☐ **cognitive behavior therapy, CBT**	**認知行動療法**

☐	cognitive consistency	認知的斉合性
☐	**cognitive dissonance theory**	**認知的不協和理論**
☐	cognitive economy	認知的経済性
☐	cognitive learning	認知学習
☐	cognitive map	認知地図
☐	cognitive neuroscience	認知神経科学
☐	cognitive process	認知過程
☐	**cognitive psychology**	**認知心理学**
☐	cognitive restructuring	認知的再構成
☐	cognitive science	認知科学
☐	cognitive therapy, CT	認知療法
☐	Cohen's κ coefficient	コーエンのカッパ係数
☐	cohesiveness	凝集性
☐	cohort analysis	コーホート分析
☐	collective goal	集団目標
☐	collective unconscious	集合的無意識
☐	collectivism	集団主義
☐	color constancy	色の恒常性
☐	color matching experiment	等色実験
☐	color rendering property	演色性
☐	commitment	コミットメント
☐	common sense psychology	常識心理学
☐	communality	共通性
☐	**communication**	**コミュニケーション**
☐	communication network	コミュニケーション・ネットワーク
☐	community	コミュニティ，地域社会
☐	companionate love	友愛
☐	**comparative psychology**	**比較心理学**
☐	compensation	補償
☐	competence	コンピタンス，能力
☐	complementary color	補色
☐	completion rate	回収率
☐	complex	コンプレックス

☐ complex cell	複雑細胞
☐ compliance	追従，応諾，コンプライアンス
☐ comprehension	理解
☐ compulsion	強迫
☐ computer assisted instruction, CAI	コンピューター支援教育
☐ computer assisted learning, CAL	コンピューター学習
☐ computer simulation	コンピューター・シミュレーション
☐ computer tomography, CT	コンピューター断層撮影
☐ **concept**	**概念**
☐ concept formation	概念形成
☐ conception	概念作用
☐ conceptual representation	概念的表象
☐ conceptualization	概念化
☐ conceptually driven processing	概念駆動型処理
☐ concrete operational stage [period]	具体的操作段階〔期〕
☐ conditioned	条件づけられた
☐ conditioned aversion	条件性嫌悪
☐ **conditioned reflex**	**条件反射**
☐ conditioned reinforcer	条件性強化子
☐ **conditioned response, CR**	**条件反応**
☐ conditioned satiety	条件性満腹感
☐ **conditioned stimulus, CS**	**条件刺激**
☐ conditioned suppression	条件性抑制
☐ **conditioning**	**条件づけ**
☐ conduct disorder	行為障害，素行症〔障害〕
☐ cone	錐体
☐ confederate	サクラ，実験協力者
☐ confidence interval	信頼区間
☐ confidentiality	守秘義務
☐ confirmation bias	確証バイアス

☐ confirmatory factor analysis, CFA	確認的因子分析
☐ **conflict**	**葛藤**, コンフリクト
☐ conflict of motives	動機の葛藤
☐ conformity	同調
☐ confound	交絡する
☐ confounding variable	交絡変数
☐ congruence	(自己)一致
☐ congruity	適合性
☐ connection	結合
☐ connectionist model	コネクショニスト・モデル
☐ connectionist network	コネクショニスト・ネットワーク
☐ connotative meaning	内包的意味
☐ conscientiousness	誠実性, 勤勉性
☐ **consciousness**	**意識**
☐ consensual validation	一致的妥当性
☐ consensus	合意性
☐ consequence	結果
☐ consequent	後件
☐ conservation	保存
☐ conservation of quantity	量の保存
☐ consistency	一貫性
☐ **constancy**	**恒常性**
☐ constant condition	恒常条件
☐ constant method	恒常法
☐ construct	構成概念
☐ construct validity	構成概念妥当性
☐ constructive perception	構成的知覚
☐ constructive process	構成的過程
☐ consumatory communication	自己充足的コミュニケーション
☐ consummatory behavior	完了的行動
☐ contemplation	関心
☐ **context**	**文脈**, コンテクスト

☐	context dependency effect	文脈依存効果
☐	contextual stimuli	文脈刺激
☐	**contingency**	**随伴性**
☐	contingency contracting	随伴性契約
☐	contingency judgement	随伴性判断
☐	contingency space	随伴性空間
☐	contingency theory	条件即応理論
☐	contingent negative variation, CNV	随伴陰性電位
☐	continuous reinforcement	連続強化
☐	continuum model	連続体モデル
☐	contraction	収縮
☐	contrast	対比
☐	contrast acuity	対比視力
☐	contrast condition	対照条件
☐	**control**	**統制, 制御**
☐	control condition	統制条件
☐	**control group**	**統制群, 対照群**
☐	control process	意図的処理〔過程〕, 統制的処理〔過程〕
☐	controllability	統制可能性, 制御可能性
☐	controlled stimulation	統制刺激
☐	convergence	輻輳
☐	convergent thinking	収束的思考
☐	convergent validity	収束的妥当性
☐	conversion disorder	変換症, 転換性障害
☐	**coping**	**コーピング, 対処**
☐	copyright	著作権
☐	Cornell Medical Index, CMI	コーネル大学健康調査票
☐	coronary heart disease, CHD	冠状動脈性心臓疾患
☐	correct rejection	コレクト・リジェクション, 正否定《信号検出理論の》
☐	**correlation**	**相関, 相関関係**
☐	**correlation coefficient**	**相関係数**

☐ correlational method	相関法
☐ correlational study	相関研究
☐ correspondence	対応性
☐ correspondent inference theory	対応推測理論
☐ cortex	皮質
☐ corticoid	コルチコイド
☐ corticosteroid	コルチコステロイド
☐ cortisol	コルチゾール
☐ **counseling**	**カウンセリング**
☐ **counterbalance**	**カウンターバランス**
☐ counterconditioning	拮抗条件づけ
☐ countertransference	逆転移
☐ couple therapy	カップル療法
☐ covariance	共分散
☐ covariance structure analysis, CSA	共分散構造分析
☐ covariate	共変数
☐ covariation principle	共変原理
☐ cover story	カバー・ストーリー
☐ **covert behavior**	**潜在行動**, あらわでない行動
☐ CR	⇨ conditioned response
☐ cranial and spinal nerves	脳脊髄神経系, 脳脊髄神経
☐ creative thinking	創造的思考
☐ creativity	創造性
☐ credit	著作権
☐ criminal psychology	犯罪心理学
☐ crisis	危機
☐ criterion related validity	基準関連妥当性
☐ criterion validity	基準妥当性, 経験的妥当性
☐ criterion variable	基準変数
☐ critical flicker frequency, CFF	臨界フリッカー周波数
☐ **critical period**	**臨界期**

☐ critical region	臨界閾
☐ cross sensitization	交絡感作
☐ cross tabulation	クロス集計
☐ cross-cultural	異文化間
☐ cross-cultural psychology	異文化間心理学，比較文化心理学
☐ cross-sectional research; cross-sectional study	横断研究
☐ crossed resistance	交絡抵抗
☐ crowd	群衆
☐ crystallized intelligence	結晶性知能
☐ CS	⇨ conditioned stimulus
☐ CT	⇨ computer tomography
☐ cue	手がかり
☐ cultural psychology	文化心理学
☐ culture-fair intelligence test	文化的に公平な知能検査
☐ curiosity	好奇心
☐ cybernetics	サイバネティックス

D

☐ d'	ディープライム《信号検出理論の》
☐ daily hassles	日常いらだち事
☐ dark adaptation	暗順応
☐ dark adaptation curve	暗順応曲線
☐ data-driven processing	データ駆動型処理
☐ daydream	白昼夢
☐ death	死
☐ death education	死への準備教育
☐ debriefing	事後説明，デブリーフィング
☐ decay theory	減衰説
☐ deception	虚偽教示，ディセプション
☐ decibel scale	デシベル尺度
☐ decision making	意思決定

☐ declarative knowledge	宣言的知識，宣言型知識
☐ declarative memory	宣言的記憶，宣言型記憶
☐ decoding	復号化，解読，デコーディング
☐ **deduction**	**演繹**
☐ deductive inference	演繹的推論
☐ deep structure	深層構造
☐ **defense mechanism**	**防衛機構，防衛機制**
☐ defensive reflex	防御反射
☐ defining feature	定義的特性
☐ degradation	分解
☐ **degree of freedom**	**自由度**
☐ deindividuation	没個性化
☐ deinstitutionalization	脱施設化
☐ delay conditioning	延滞条件づけ
☐ delinquency	非行
☐ delirium	せん妄
☐ delusion	妄想
☐ demagogy	デマ
☐ demand	要求
☐ demand characteristics	要求特性
☐ dementia	認知症
☐ dendrite	樹状突起
☐ denial	否認，現実否認
☐ denotative meaning	外延的意味，指示的意味
☐ dependency	依存性，依存症
☐ **dependent variable**	**従属変数**
☐ depressants	抑制薬
☐ **depression**	**うつ病，抑うつ**
☐ depressive disorder	うつ病性障害，抑うつ障害
☐ deprivation	剥奪
☐ depth cue	奥行き手がかり
☐ depth perception	奥行知覚
☐ derived motive	派生的動機

☐	descending series	下降系列
☐	descending trial	下降試行
☐	**descriptive statistics**	**記述統計(量)，記述統計学**
☐	desensitization	脱感作
☐	**desire**	**欲望**
☐	detection of deception	虚偽検出
☐	**development**	**発達**
☐	development(al) acceleration	発達加速現象
☐	developmental disorder	発達症〔障害〕
☐	**developmental psychology**	**発達心理学**
☐	deviant behavior	逸脱行動
☐	deviation	偏差
☐	deviation IQ	偏差知能指数
☐	diagnosis	診断
☐	Diagnostic and Statistical Manual of Mental Disorders, DSM	精神疾患の診断・統計マニュアル，DSM
☐	diastolic blood pressure, DBP	拡張期血圧
☐	dichotic listening	両耳分離聴
☐	dichromatism	二色型色覚
☐	diencephalon	間脳
☐	difference〔differential〕limen; difference〔differential〕threshold	弁別閾
☐	differential probability principle	差異的確率の原理
☐	differential reinforcement	分化強化
☐	differential reinforcement of low rate, DRL	低反応率分化強化スケジュール
☐	differentiation	分化
☐	diffusion of responsibility	責任の分散，責任の拡散
☐	digestion	消化
☐	dilemma	ジレンマ
☐	dimension	次元

☐ direct observation	直接観察	
☐ direct proportion	正比例	
☐ directed thinking	目標的思考, 目標づけられた思考	
☐ discrete trial	離散試行	
☐ **discrimination**	**弁別**	
☐ discrimination reaction time, DRT	弁別反応時間	
☐ discriminative stimulus	弁別刺激	
☐ discriminative threshold	弁別閾	
☐ **discussion**	**考察, 議論, 論議**	
☐ disease model	疾病モデル	
☐ dishabituation	脱馴化, 脱慣れ	
☐ disinhibition	脱抑制	
☐ displacement	置き換え	
☐ display rule	表示規則	
☐ disposition	気質, 傾(向)性	
☐ dispositional attribution	属性(への)帰属	
☐ dissociation	解離	
☐ dissociative disorder	解離性症〔障害〕	
☐ dissociative identity disorder	解離性同一性症〔障害〕	
☐ distal stimulus	遠隔刺激	
☐ distinctiveness	弁別性	
☐ distraction	注意の逸脱, かく乱	
☐ distractor	ディストラクター	
☐ distress	苦痛	
☐ distributed learning	分散学習	
☐ distribution	分布	
☐ divergent thinking	拡散的思考, 発散的思考	
☐ divided attention	分配的注意	
☐ dizygotic twins	二卵性双生児	
☐ domain	領域, 次元	
☐ door-in-the-face-technique	譲歩的要請法, ドア・イン・ザ・フェイス法	

☐ dopamine	ドーパミン
☐ double barreled question	ダブルバーレル質問
☐ **double-blind test 〔design; procedure; technique〕**	**二重盲検法**
☐ Down syndrome	ダウン症候群
☐ dream analysis	夢分析
☐ drift	ドリフト，逸脱
☐ **drive**	**動因**
☐ drive reduction	動因低減
☐ drive reduction theory	動因低減説
☐ drive theory	動因理論
☐ drowsiness	まどろみ，眠気
☐ drug abuse	薬物乱用
☐ drug dependence	薬物依存
☐ DSM	⇨ Diagnostic and Statistical Manual of Mental Disorders
☐ dual coding hypothesis	二重符号化仮説
☐ dual task	二重作業，二重課題
☐ dualism	二元論，心身二元論
☐ dynamic control theory	力学的制御理論
☐ dynamic perception	動的知覚
☐ dynamic psychotherapy	力動的心理療法
☐ dysarthria	運動性構音障害
☐ dysfunction	機能不全
☐ dyskinesia	運動障害
☐ dyslexia	読字障害

E

☐ E	⇨ experimenter
☐ eardrum	鼓膜
☐ early childhood	幼児期
☐ early experience	初期経験

☐ eating disorder	摂食障害	
☐ ECG	⇨ electrocardiogram	
☐ echoic memory	エコイックメモリー，音響記憶	
☐ echolalia	反響言語	
☐ eclectic approach	折衷的アプローチ	
☐ ecological niche	生態的地位	
☐ ecological optics	生態光学	
☐ ecological self	生態学的自己	
☐ ecological validity	生態学的妥当性	
☐ educational gerontology	教育老年学	
☐ educational psychology	教育心理学	
☐ EEG	⇨ electroencephalogram	
☐ effect size	効果量	
☐ effector	効果器	
☐ efferent nerve	遠心性神経	
☐ efficacy expectancy	効力予測	
☐ **ego**	**自我，エゴ**	
☐ egocentric speech	自己中心的発話，自己中心語	
☐ egocentric thinking	自己中心的思考	
☐ egocentrism	自己中心性	
☐ eidetic image	直観像	
☐ elaboration	精緻化	
☐ elaboration likelihood model	精緻化見込みモデル	
☐ elaborative rehearsal	精緻化リハーサル	
☐ Electra complex	エレクトラ・コンプレックス	
☐ electric shock	電撃，電気ショック	
☐ electrical brain activity	脳電気活動	
☐ electrocardiogram, ECG	心電図	
☐ electroconvulsive therapy, ECT	電気けいれん療法	
☐ electrode	電極	
☐ electrodermal activity, EDA	皮膚電気活動	
☐ electrodermal reflex	皮膚電気反射	

☐ **electroencephalogram, EEG**	**脳波**，脳電図
☐ electromyogram, EMG	筋電図
☐ electrooculogram, EOG	眼電図
☐ elementalism	要素主義
☐ emergency reaction	危急反応
☐ EMG	⇨ electromyogram
☐ **emotion**	**情動**，情緒，感情
☐ emotion-focused coping	情動焦点型コーピング
☐ emotion regulation	情動制御，感情調整
☐ emotional conditioning	情動条件づけ
☐ emotional eating	情動摂食
☐ emotional intelligence	情動知能
☐ emotional response	情動反応
☐ emotional stability	情緒安定性
☐ emotional valence	情動価
☐ empathy	共感(性)
☐ empirical study	実証的研究
☐ empiricism	経験主義
☐ encephalization	大脳化
☐ encoding	符号化
☐ encoding-shift hypothesis	符号化移行仮説
☐ encoding specificity principle	符号化特性原理
☐ encoding stage	符号化段階
☐ encounter group	エンカウンター・グループ
☐ endocrine	内分泌
☐ endogenous potentials	内因性電位
☐ endogenous psychosis	内因性精神病
☐ engagement	関与
☐ engineering psychology	工学心理学
☐ **environment**	**環境**
☐ environmental variable	環境変数
☐ environmentalism	環境主義
☐ EOG	⇨ electrooculogram

☐ epidemiology	疫学
☐ epilepsy	てんかん
☐ epinephrine	エピネフリン《＝アドレナリン》
☐ episode	エピソード
☐ **episodic memory**	**エピソード記憶**
☐ equilibrium theory	均衡理論
☐ equipotentiality	等価性
☐ equity theory	公平〔衡平〕理論
☐ ergonomics	人間工学, エルゴノミクス
☐ Eros	エロス
☐ ERP	⇨ event-related brain potential
☐ **error**	**誤差**
☐ error back propagation learning rule	誤差逆伝播学習則
☐ error of type I	第1種の誤り〔過誤〕
☐ error of type II	第2種の誤り〔過誤〕
☐ es	エス《イドと同じ》
☐ **escape**	**逃避**
☐ escape behavior	逃避行動
☐ escape learning	逃避学習
☐ ESP	⇨ extrasensory perception
☐ ethical standards	倫理基準
☐ **ethics**	**倫理(学)**
☐ ethnocentrism	自民族中心主義
☐ ethologist	動物行動学者, 行動生物学者
☐ ethology	動物行動学, 行動生物学
☐ eugenics	優生学
☐ euphemism	婉曲表現
☐ evaluation	評価
☐ evaluation apprehension	評価懸念
☐ **event-related (brain) potential, ERP**	**事象関連(脳)電位**
☐ event schema	事象スキーマ

☐ everyday memory	日常記憶
☐ **evidence**	**根拠**, 証拠
☐ evocative interaction	喚起性相互作用
☐ evoked potential, EP	誘発電位, 感覚誘発電位
☐ evolutionary psychology	進化心理学
☐ excitation	興奮, 発揚
☐ excitatory conditioning	興奮条件づけ
☐ excitatory connections	興奮性結合
☐ excitement	興奮
☐ existential therapy	実存療法
☐ exogenous potentials	外因性電位
☐ expectancy theory	予期説
☐ **expectation**	**期待**, 予期
☐ expected frequency	期待度数
☐ **experiment**	**実験**
☐ experimental analysis of behavior	実験的行動分析
☐ experimental condition	実験条件
☐ experimental control	実験的統制, 実験制御
☐ experimental design	実験計画
☐ **experimental group**	**実験群**
☐ experimental method	実験法
☐ experimental observation	実験観察法
☐ **experimental psychology**	**実験心理学**
☐ **experimenter**	**実験者**
☐ experimenter effect	実験者効果
☐ expertize	熟達(化)
☐ explicit memory	顕在記憶
☐ exploratory data analysis, EDA	探索的データ解析
☐ exploratory factor analysis, EFA	探索的因子分析
☐ exposure therapy	暴露療法
☐ expression	表出

☐ extensional meaning	指示的意味
☐ external control	外的統制
☐ external validity	外的妥当性
☐ **extinction**	**消去**
☐ extraneous variable	剰余変数
☐ extrapunitive response	外罰的反応
☐ extrasensory perception, ESP	超感覚的知覚, 超能力
☐ **extraversion; extroversion**	**外向性**
☐ extrovert	外向型
☐ eye contact	アイコンタクト
☐ eye fixation-related potential	眼球停留関連電位
☐ **eye movement**	**眼球運動**
☐ eyeblink	瞬目
☐ eyelid reflex	眼瞼反射
☐ eyewitness testimony	目撃証言

F

☐ F test	F検定
☐ face sheet	フェイスシート
☐ face-to-face group	対面集団
☐ face validity	表面的妥当性
☐ facet	下位次元, 側面, ファセット
☐ **facial expression**	**表情**
☐ facial feedback hypothesis	顔面フィードバック仮説
☐ facilitation	促進
☐ **factor**	**因子, 要因**
☐ **factor analysis**	**因子分析**
☐ factorial design	要因計画
☐ false alarm, FA	誤報, フォルス・アラーム《信号検出理論の》
☐ false-alarms rate	フォルス・アラーム率
☐ false memory	虚偽記憶

☐ false recognition	虚再認
☐ falsification	反証
☐ familiarity	熟知度，親近性
☐ family therapy	家族療法
☐ fantasy	空想
☐ fashion	流行
☐ fast Fourier transform, FFT	高速フーリエ変換，ＦＦＴ法
☐ fatigue	疲労
☐ **fear**	**恐れ，恐怖**
☐ fear conditioning	恐怖条件づけ
☐ feasibility	実行可能性
☐ feature	素性，特徴
☐ feature comparison model	特性比較モデル
☐ feature integration theory	特徴統合理論
☐ Fechner's law	フェヒナーの法則
☐ feedback	フィードバック
☐ feeding center	摂食中枢
☐ **feeling**	**感情**
☐ feeling of knowing	既知感
☐ femininity	女性性
☐ feral child	野生児
☐ fetal period	胎児期
☐ field dependence	場依存性
☐ field experiment	フィールド実験，現場実験
☐ field theory	場の理論
☐ fight-or-flight response	闘争・逃走反応
☐ fighting	闘争
☐ figurative language	比喩
☐ figure	図
☐ figure-ground	図と地
☐ filial imprinting	子の刻印づけ，子の刷り込み
☐ finger temperature	指先〔尖〕温
☐ first impression	第一印象

☐ first word	初語
☐ Fisher's exact test	フィッシャーの正確〔直接〕確率検定
☐ fixation	固着, 凝視, 固視
☐ fixation pause	眼球停留
☐ fixation point	注視点, 固視点
☐ fixed action pattern, FAP	恒常的動作パターン
☐ fixed effect	固定効果
☐ fixed interval schedule	固定間隔スケジュール
☐ fixed ratio schedule	固定比率スケジュール
☐ fixed role therapy	役割固定法
☐ flashback	フラッシュバック
☐ flashbulb memory	フラッシュバルブ記憶, 閃光記憶
☐ fleeing	逃走
☐ flicker test	フリッカーテスト
☐ flooding	フラッディング法, フラッディング
☐ floor effect	床効果
☐ flow theory	フロー理論
☐ flowchart model	フローチャート・モデル
☐ fluid intelligence	流動性知能
☐ fMRI	⇨ functional magnetic resonance imaging
☐ focusing	フォーカシング
☐ follow-up study	追跡研究
☐ follower	フォロワー, 追従者
☐ food history	食物歴
☐ food preference	食物嗜好
☐ foot-in-the-door technique	段階的要請法, フット・イン・ザ・ドア・テクニック
☐ forced-choice method	強制選択法
☐ **forgetting**	**忘却**
☐ formal	フォーマル, 形式, 公式
☐ formal group	公式集団
☐ formal norm	公式な規範

☐ formal operational stage〔period〕	形式的操作段階〔期〕
☐ fornix	脳梁
☐ forward masking	順向性マスキング
☐ fovea	中心窩
☐ frame of reference	準拠枠
☐ free association	自由連想(法)
☐ free operant	フリーオペラント，自由オペラント
☐ free recall	自由再生
☐ free response	自由反応
☐ free rider	フリーライダー，ただのり
☐ free-running rhythm	自由継続リズム
☐ frequency	周波数，度数
☐ **frequency distribution**	**度数分布**
☐ Freudian slip	フロイト的言い間違い
☐ frontal lobe	前頭葉
☐ frontal midline theta, Fm θ	前頭正中部 θ 波
☐ **frustration**	**欲求不満，フラストレーション**
☐ frustration-aggression hypothesis	欲求不満攻撃仮説
☐ frustration tolerance	欲求不満耐性
☐ function	機能，関数
☐ functional asymmetry	機能的非対称性
☐ functional autonomy	機能的自律性
☐ functional fixedness	機能的固定，機能的固着
☐ functional localization	機能局在
☐ functional magnetic resonance imaging, fMRI	機能的磁気共鳴画像
☐ functional specialization theory	機能特殊化説
☐ **functionalism**	**機能主義**
☐ fundamental attribution error	基本的な帰属の誤り

G	
☐ g factor	⇨ general (intelligence) factor
☐ galvanic skin response, GSR	皮膚電気反応
☐ gambler's fallacy	ギャンブラーの錯誤〔誤謬〕
☐ gang age	ギャングエイジ
☐ ganglia（単数：ganglion）	神経節
☐ ganzfeld procedure	ガンツフェルト法
☐ Gardner's theory of multiple intelligence	ガードナー多重知能理論
☐ gastric motility	胃運動性
☐ gate control theory of pain	痛みのゲートコントロール理論，痛みの関門制御理論
☐ gaze	凝視
☐ gemeinschaft	ゲマインシャフト
☐ **gender**	**ジェンダー**，**性**
☐ gender identity disorder	性同一性障害
☐ gender schema	ジェンダー・スキーマ
☐ **gene**	**遺伝子**
☐ general adaptive syndrome, GAS	汎適応症候群，一般適応症候群
☐ general context effect	一般的文脈効果
☐ general (intelligence) factor; g factor	一般（知能）因子
☐ General Health Questionnaire, GHQ	精神健康調査票
☐ general paresis	進行マヒ
☐ general slowing model	普遍的遅延モデル，一般遅延モデル
☐ **generalization**	**般化**，**一般化**
☐ generalization gradient	般化勾配
☐ generalized anxiety disorder	全般不安症，全般性不安障害
☐ generation effect	生成効果
☐ generative grammar	生成文法
☐ genetic factor	遺伝的要因
☐ genetic polymorphism	遺伝子多型

☐ genital stage	性器期
☐ genotype	遺伝子型
☐ genuineness	真実性，純粋性
☐ geriatric depression scale, GDS	老人用うつスケール
☐ gerontology	老年学
☐ gesellschaft	ゲゼルシャフト
☐ Gestalt	ゲシュタルト
☐ **Gestalt psychology**	**ゲシュタルト心理学**，形態心理学
☐ Gestalt therapy	ゲシュタルト療法
☐ GHQ	⇨ General Health Questionnaire
☐ gifted	天才，ギフテッド
☐ gland	腺
☐ glia cells	グリア細胞
☐ goal	目標
☐ Golgi's method	ゴルジ染色
☐ good-poor analysis; G-P analysis	上位・下位分析
☐ grain size	きめの細かさ
☐ grammar	文法
☐ grammatical morpheme	文法形態素
☐ grasping reflex	把握反射
☐ gray〔grey〕matter	灰白質
☐ ground	根拠，地
☐ **group**	**集団，群**，グループ
☐ group cohesiveness	集団凝集性
☐ group dynamics	グループダイナミックス，集団力学
☐ group experiment	集団実験
☐ group norm	集団規範
☐ group polarization effect	集団極性化効果
☐ group pressure	集団圧力
☐ group therapy	集団療法
☐ grouping by proximity	近接による群化
☐ grouping by similarity	類同による群化

☐ groupthink	集団思考
☐ GSR	⇨ galvanic skin response
☐ gustation	味覚

H

☐ habit	習慣
☐ habit strength	習慣強度
☐ **habituation**	**馴化**
☐ habituation-dishabituation technique	馴化・脱馴化法
☐ habituation effect	馴化効果, 慣れの効果
☐ habituation method	馴化法
☐ hair cells	有毛細胞
☐ halfway house	中間施設
☐ **hallucination**	**幻覚**
☐ hallucinogen	幻覚薬
☐ halo-effect	光背効果, ハロー効果
☐ hardiness	強靭さ, ハーディネス
☐ hardy personality	ハーディネス・パーソナリティ特性
☐ Hawthorne research	ホーソン研究
☐ head injury	頭部外傷
☐ health behavior	健康行動
☐ health belief model	健康信念モデル
☐ health care system	ヘルスケアシステム
☐ health practices	健康習慣
☐ health protective behavior	予防的健康行動
☐ health psychology	健康心理学
☐ health-related behavior	健康関連行動
☐ health sciences	健康科学
☐ healthism	健康主義
☐ heart beat	心拍
☐ **heart rate, HR**	**心拍数**, 心拍率

☐ heart rate variability, HRV	心拍(率)変動
☐ Hebbian rule	ヘッブの法則，ヘブ則
☐ hedonic value	快をもたらす程度，感情価
☐ help seeking behavior	求援助行動
☐ helping behavior	援助行動
☐ hemisphere	半球
☐ heredity	遺伝
☐ heritability	遺伝規定性
☐ heroin	ヘロイン
☐ hertz, Hz	ヘルツ
☐ **heuristic**	**ヒューリスティック**
☐ hidden observer	隠れた観察者
☐ hierarchical network model	階層的ネットワーク・モデル
☐ hierarchy of fear	不安階層(表)
☐ hierarchy of needs	欲求階層説
☐ higher-order conditioning	高次条件づけ
☐ hippocampus	海馬
☐ hit	ヒット，的中《信号検出理論の》
☐ hit rate	ヒット率《信号検出理論の》
☐ holism〔wholism〕	全体論
☐ holistic thought	全体論的思考
☐ **homeostasis**	**ホメオスタシス**，生理的平衡，生体恒常性，恒常性
☐ homeostatic sleep drive	生体恒常的睡眠動因
☐ homogeneity	同質性
☐ horizontal axis	横軸
☐ horizontal eye movement	水平眼球運動
☐ **hormone**	**ホルモン**
☐ hospice	ホスピス
☐ hospitalism	ホスピタリズム
☐ hostile aggression	敵意ある攻撃性
☐ hostility	敵意
☐ HR	⇨ heart rate

☐ hue	色相
☐ human factors	人間工学
☐ humanist	人間主義者，ヒューマニスト
☐ humanistic psychology	ヒューマニスティック心理学，人間性心理学
☐ humanistic therapy	人間性療法
☐ humorism	四体液説
☐ hunger	飢え，飢餓
☐ hunger pang	飢餓感固有の痛み
☐ Huntington's disease	ハンチントン病
☐ hybrid	ハイブリッド
☐ hyperactivity	多動性
☐ **hypnosis**	**催眠**
☐ hypnotic suggestion	催眠暗示
☐ hypochondriasis	心気症
☐ hypothalamus	視床下部
☐ **hypothesis**（複数：**hypotheses**）	**仮説**
☐ hypothesis verification	仮説検証
☐ hypothetical construct	仮説的構成概念
☐ hypothetico-deductive method	仮説演繹法
☐ hysteria	ヒステリー
☐ Hz	⇨ hertz

I

☐ iconic memory	アイコニックメモリー，画像記憶
☐ **id**	**イド**《エスと同じ》
☐ identical twins	一卵性双生児
☐ identification	同一化
☐ **identity**	**自我同一性，アイデンティティ**
☐ identity diffusion	自我同一性の拡散，アイデンティティ拡散

☐ ideology	イデオロギー
☐ ideomotor action	観念運動
☐ illness behavior	病気行動
☐ illuminance	照度
☐ **illusion**	**錯覚**
☐ illusory conjunction	錯覚的結合
☐ **image; imagery**	**心像**, イメージ
☐ imaginal thought	イメージ的思考
☐ imbalance	不均衡状態
☐ imitation	模倣
☐ immediate memory	直後記憶
☐ immediate memory span	直接記憶範囲
☐ immediate reinforcement	直後強化
☐ immune	免疫
☐ immune system	免疫系
☐ impact evaluation	インパクト評価
☐ implicit leaning	潜在学習
☐ implicit memory	潜在記憶
☐ **impression**	**印象**
☐ impression formation	印象形成
☐ impression management	印象操作
☐ **imprinting**	**刻印づけ**, 刷り込み, インプリンティング
☐ impulse	インパルス, 衝動
☐ impulsiveness	衝動性
☐ impunitive response	無罰的反応
☐ in-group	内集団
☐ in vitro measurement	生体外測定法, 試験管内測定
☐ in vivo exposure	現実暴露法
☐ in vivo measurement	生体内測定法
☐ **incentive**	**誘因**
☐ incentive motivation	誘因動機づけ
☐ incidence	発生率

☐ incidental learning	偶発学習	
☐ incubation effect	孵化効果	
☐ **independent variable**	**独立変数**	
☐ **individual difference**	**個人差，個体差**	
☐ individualism	個人主義	
☐ individuality	個体内変動，個性	
☐ individualization	個性化	
☐ individuation	個別化，個性化，個体化	
☐ induced motion	誘導運動	
☐ **induction**	**帰納**，誘導	
☐ inductive reasoning	帰納推理	
☐ industrial psychology	産業心理学	
☐ **infancy**	**幼児期，乳児期**	
☐ **infant**	**幼児，乳児，乳幼児**	
☐ **inference**	**推論**，推理	
☐ **inferential statistics**	**推測統計**，推測統計学	
☐ inferiority	劣等感	
☐ informal	インフォーマル，非公式	
☐ informal group	非公式集団，インフォーマルグループ	
☐ informal norm	非公式な規範	
☐ information	情報	
☐ **information processing**	**情報処理**	
☐ information-processing model	情報処理モデル	
☐ information theory	情報理論	
☐ informational power	情報勢力	
☐ **informed consent**	**インフォームド・コンセント**，説明を受けた上での承諾	
☐ infradian rhythm	インフラディアン・リズム，長日周期	
☐ ingratiation	迎合行動	
☐ ingrowth stage	内言化段階	
☐ inherited characteristics	遺伝形質〔特性〕	
☐ **inhibition**	**制止，抑制**	

☐ inhibitor	制止子，抑制子	
☐ inhibitory conditioning	制止条件づけ，抑制条件づけ	
☐ inhibitory connections	抑制性結合	
☐ inkblot	インクのしみ，インクブロット	
☐ innate behavior	生得的行動	
☐ innate releasing mechanism, IRM	生得的触発機構	
☐ inner speech	内言	
☐ innervation	神経支配	
☐ inoculation theory	接種理論	
☐ **insight**	**洞察，見通し**	
☐ insight therapy	洞察療法	
☐ insomnia	不眠症	
☐ inspection task	検査作業	
☐ instance	事例	
☐ **instinct**	**本能，欲動**	
☐ instinctive behavior	本能的行動	
☐ instinctive drift	本能的逸脱，本能的漂流	
☐ **instruction**	**教示，インストラクション**	
☐ instrumental aggression	手段としての攻撃性，道具的攻撃	
☐ **instrumental conditioning**	**道具的条件づけ**	
☐ instrumental learning	道具的学習	
☐ intake interview	受理面接，インテーク面接	
☐ intellectualization	知性化	
☐ **intelligence**	**知能，知性**	
☐ intelligence quotient, IQ	知能指数	
☐ intelligence test	知能検査	
☐ **intensity**	**強度，強さ**	
☐ intention	意図	
☐ intentionality	志向性	
☐ **interaction**	**相互作用，交互作用**	
☐ interaction effect	交互作用効果	

☐ interactional process analysis, IPA	相互作用過程分析
☐ interbeat interval, IBI	心拍間隔，拍動間隔
☐ interdependency	相互依存性
☐ **interference**	**干渉**
☐ interference theory	干渉説
☐ interfering variable	干渉変数
☐ interjudge reliability	判断者間信頼性
☐ intermittent reinforcement	間欠強化
☐ internal conflict	内的葛藤
☐ internal consistency	内的一貫性，内的整合性
☐ internal control	内的統制
☐ internal desynchronization	内的脱同調
☐ internal validity	内的妥当性
☐ internalization	内在化
☐ interobserver reliability	観察者間信頼性
☐ interpersonal attraction	対人魅力
☐ interpersonal cognition	対人認知
☐ interpersonal repulsion	対人的回避
☐ interpersonal skill	対人スキル
☐ interpersonal theory	対人関係論
☐ interpersonal therapy	対人関係療法
☐ interposition	重なり《奥行き知覚の》，介入
☐ interpretation	解釈
☐ interpsychic	精神間，相互心理的
☐ interrater agreement	評定者間一致度
☐ interrater reliability	評定者間信頼性
☐ interresponse time, IRT	反応間間隔
☐ interstimulus interval, ISI	刺激間間隔
☐ intertrial interval, ITI	試行(間)間隔
☐ interval estimation	区間推定(法)
☐ interval scale	間隔尺度
☐ interval schedule	間隔スケジュール

☐ intervening variable	媒介変数
☐ intervention study	介入研究
☐ **interview**	**面接**
☐ interview for diagnosis	診断的面接
☐ interview technique	面接法
☐ intimacy	親密性
☐ intrapsychic	精神内の
☐ intra sleep cycle	睡眠内周期
☐ intrinsic motivation	内発的動機づけ
☐ **introduction**	**序論，導入(部)**
☐ intropunitive response	内罰的反応
☐ **introspection**	**内省，内観**
☐ **introversion**	**内向性**
☐ introvert	内向型
☐ intuition	直観
☐ inventory	目録，質問紙
☐ inverse proportion	反比例
☐ involuntary activity	不随意活動
☐ involuntary response	無意図的反応
☐ ion channel	イオンチャネル
☐ IQ	⇨ intelligence quotient
☐ iris	虹彩
☐ irrational belief	非合理な信念
☐ irregular sleep	不規則的睡眠
☐ isolation	隔離
☐ item analysis	項目分析
☐ item characteristic curve	項目特性曲線
☐ item response theory, IRT	項目反応理論，項目応答理論
☐ ITI	⇨ intertrial interval

J

☐ **James-Lange theory**	**ジェームズ゠ランゲ説**

☐ just noticeable difference, jnd	丁度可知差異

K

☐ kinesthesis	運動感覚
☐ knowledge	知識
☐ knowledge of performance, KP	遂行の知識
☐ knowledge of result, KR	結果の知識

L

☐ labeling effect	ラベリング効果
☐ laboratory experiment	実験室実験
☐ lambda complex	ラムダ〔λ〕複合
☐ lambda response	ラムダ反応
☐ language	言語
☐ language acquisition device	(生得的)言語獲得装置
☐ language disorder	言語症〔障害〕
☐ late positive component, LPC	後期陽性成分
☐ latency	潜時
☐ latency period	潜伏期
☐ latent content	潜在内容
☐ latent learning	潜在学習
☐ lateral geniculate body, LGB	外側膝状体
☐ lateral hypothalamus	外側視床下部《摂食中枢》
☐ lateral inhibition	側抑制
☐ law of causality	因果法則,因果律
☐ law of contiguity	接近の法則
☐ law of effect	効果の法則
☐ law of large numbers	大数の法則
☐ law of parsimony	節約の法則
☐ law of Prägnanz	プレグナンツの法則
☐ law of small numbers	少数の法則

☐ LD	⇨ learning disabilities; learning disorders
☐ leader	リーダー
☐ leadership	リーダーシップ
☐ leading question	誘導質問，誘導尋問
☐ **learned helplessness**	**学習性(の)無力感，学習性絶望**
☐ learned irrelevance	無関係性の学習
☐ **learning**	**学習**
☐ learning curve	学習曲線
☐ **learning disability; learning disorder, LD**	**学習症〔障害〕**
☐ learning set	学習の構え，学習セット
☐ legitimate power	正当勢力
☐ level	水準
☐ level of aspiration	要求水準
☐ level of significance	有意水準
☐ levels of processing	処理水準
☐ lexical decision task	語彙判断課題
☐ libido	リビドー
☐ **lie detection**	**嘘発見**
☐ lie detector	嘘発見器
☐ life event	生活上の出来事，ライフイベント
☐ life instinct	生の本能
☐ Life Satisfaction Index, LSI	人生満足度尺度
☐ lifespan development	生涯発達
☐ lifetime prevalence rate	生涯有病率
☐ light adaptation	明順応
☐ lightness	明度
☐ Likert scaling	リッカート法
☐ liking	好意
☐ limbic system	大脳辺縁系，辺縁系
☐ limen	閾
☐ linear	直線形，線型

☐ linguistics	言語学	
☐ linguistic acquisition device	言語習得装置	
☐ linguistic relativity hypothesis	言語相対性仮説	
☐ linguistic universal	言語普遍性	
☐ link	環	
☐ literacy	リテラシー	
☐ literature review	文献研究	
☐ living will	生前の意思表示書，リビングウィル	
☐ Lloyd Morgan's canon	モーガンの公準	
☐ lobe	葉《脳などの》	
☐ lobotomy	ロボトミー	
☐ locus of control, LOC	統制の所在，統制の位置	
☐ logic	論理	
☐ logotherapy	ロゴテラピー，実存分析	
☐ long-term depression	長期抑圧	
☐ **long-term memory, LTM**	**長期記憶**	
☐ long-term potentiation	長期増強	
☐ long-term store, LTS	長期貯蔵庫	
☐ **longitudinal research**; longitudinal study	**縦断研究**	
☐ loosening of associations	連合弛緩	
☐ loudness	音の大きさ	
☐ love	愛情	
☐ low-ball technique	承諾先取り法，承諾先取要請法，ロー・ボール・テクニック	
☐ LTM	⇨ long-term memory	
☐ lucid dream	明晰夢	
☐ luminance	輝度	

M

☐ Mach band	マッハバンド，マッハの帯

☐ magazine training	マガジン訓練,給仕装置への馴致訓練
☐ magnetic resonance imaging, MRI	磁気共鳴断層撮影,磁気共鳴画像,核磁気共鳴画像診断
☐ magneto-evoked potential	磁気誘発電位
☐ magnetoencephalogram, MEG	脳磁図
☐ magnitude estimation	マグニチュード推定法
☐ mail survey	郵送調査
☐ main effect	主効果
☐ maintenance	維持
☐ maintenance rehearsal	維持リハーサル
☐ major 〔unipolar〕 depression	大〔単極性〕うつ病
☐ majority	大多数者集団,マジョリティ
☐ maladaptive behavior	不適応行動
☐ managerial grid	マネジリアル・グリッド
☐ mania	躁病,マニア
☐ manic-depressive illness	躁うつ病
☐ manic-depressive psychosis	躁うつ精神病
☐ manic state	躁状態
☐ Manifest Anxiety Scale, MAS	顕在性不安尺度
☐ manifest content	顕在内容
☐ **manipulation**	**操作**
☐ marijuana	マリファナ
☐ marital therapy	夫婦療法
☐ masculinity	男性性
☐ masking	マスキング
☐ masking effect	マスキング効果
☐ massed learning	集中学習
☐ material	(実験)材料
☐ materialism	物質主義
☐ maternal deprivation	マターナル・デプリベーション,母性剥奪
☐ **maturation, maturity**	**成熟**

☐ Maudsley Personality Inventory, MPI	モーズレー人格目録
☐ maximum entropy method, MEM	最大エントロピー法
☐ maximum likelihood method, MLM	最尤法，ML法
☐ McGurk effect	マガーク効果
☐ MDS	⇨ multi-dimensional scale
☐ **mean**	**平均(値)**
☐ mean order	平均順位
☐ meaning	意味
☐ means-ends analysis	手段・目標分析
☐ **measure**	**測度**
☐ **measurement**	**測定**
☐ mechanics	メカニクス
☐ mechanism	メカニズム，機械論
☐ medial geniculate body	内側膝状体
☐ **median**	**中央値**
☐ mediation	媒介
☐ mediation theory	媒介理論
☐ mediator	媒介体
☐ medical [disease] model	医学[疾病]モデル
☐ meditation	瞑想
☐ medulla	延髄
☐ MEG	⇨ magnetoencephalogram
☐ mel scale	メル尺度
☐ melatonin	メラトニン
☐ member	成員，メンバー
☐ memorization	記銘
☐ **memory**	**記憶**
☐ memory load	記憶負荷
☐ memory span	記憶範囲
☐ memory strategy	記憶方略
☐ memory trace	記憶痕跡

☐ menarche	初潮	
☐ mental activity	心的活動, 精神活動	
☐ mental age, MA	精神年齢	
☐ mental chronometry	精神時間測定法	
☐ mental disorder	精神疾患, 精神障害	
☐ mental health	精神的健康, 精神衛生	
☐ mental image	心像, 心的イメージ	
☐ mental model	メンタルモデル	
☐ mental process	心的過程, 精神過程	
☐ mental representation	心的表象	
☐ mental retardation	精神遅滞	
☐ mental rotation	心的回転	
☐ mental workload	心的負荷, 精神負荷	
☐ mentally retarded	精神遅滞者	
☐ mere exposure effect	単純接触効果	
☐ mesencephalon	中脳	
☐ meta analysis	メタ分析	
☐ metacognition	メタ認知	
☐ metacontrast	メタコントラスト	
☐ metaphor	隠喩, メタファー, 比喩	
☐ methadone	メタドン	
☐ method	**方法**	
☐ method of adjustment	調整法	
☐ method of limits	極限法	
☐ method of loci	場所法	
☐ method of paired comparisons	一対比較法	
☐ method of successive approximation	漸次的接近法	
☐ metonymy	換喩	
☐ midbrain	中脳	
☐ middle ear	中耳	
☐ minimal brain damage	微細脳損傷	

☐ Mini-Mental State Examination, MMSE	ミニメンタル・ステート検査	
☐ Minnesota Multiphasic Personality Inventory, MMPI	ミネソタ多面的人格目録	
☐ minority	少数者集団, マイノリティ	
☐ minority influence	少数派の影響	
☐ mirror drawing	鏡映描写	
☐ misattribution	錯誤帰属, 誤帰属	
☐ mismatch negativity, MMN	ミスマッチ陰性電位, ミスマッチ・ネガティビティ	
☐ miss	ミス《信号検出理論の》	
☐ MMPI	⇨ Minnesota Multiphasic Personality Inventory	
☐ M'Naghten Rule	マクノーテン裁定	
☐ mnemonics	記憶術	
☐ mob	モッブ, 暴集	
☐ modality	モダリティ, 感覚様相	
☐ **mode**	**最頻値**	
☐ **modeling**	**モデリング**	
☐ moderator variable	調整変数	
☐ molar behavior	全体的行動	
☐ molecular behavior	分子的〔微視的〕行動	
☐ monoamine oxidase, MAO	モノアミン酸化酵素	
☐ monochromatism	一色型色覚	
☐ monozygotic twins	一卵性双生児	
☐ **mood**	**気分**	
☐ mood congruency effect	気分一致効果	
☐ mood disorder	気分障害	
☐ mood state dependency effect	気分状態依存効果	
☐ moral judgment	道徳的判断	
☐ morale	モラール, 士気	
☐ moratorium	モラトリアム, 猶予期間	
☐ Morgan's canon	モーガンの公準	
☐ Moro reflex	モロー反射	

☐ morpheme	形態素
☐ motherese	育児語
☐ motion parallax	運動視差
☐ **motivation**	**動機づけ**
☐ motive	動機
☐ motor cortex	運動皮質
☐ motor nerve	運動神経
☐ motor potential	運動電位
☐ motor unit	運動単位
☐ **movement**	**運動**
☐ MRI	⇨ magnetic resonance imaging
☐ Müller-Lyer illusion	ミューラー・リヤー錯視
☐ multi-dimensional scale, MDS	多次元尺度構成法
☐ multimodal attention	多感覚様相的注意
☐ multiple answer	複数回答法
☐ multiple-baseline design	多元ベースライン計画法
☐ multiple choice method	多肢選択法
☐ multiple comparison	多重比較
☐ multiple intelligence, MI	多重知能
☐ multiple measurement	多重測定
☐ multiple operation	多重操作
☐ multiple personality	多重人格
☐ multiple regression analysis	重回帰分析
☐ multiple T-maze	複合T迷路
☐ multistore model	多重貯蔵モデル
☐ multivariate analysis	多変量解析
☐ multivariate experiment	多変量実験
☐ Munsell system	マンセル表色系
☐ muscle	筋, 筋肉
☐ muscle potential	筋電位
☐ music therapy	音楽療法
☐ mutism	緘黙, 無言症

N

☐ N2-P3 complex	N2-P3複合
☐ N400	エヌ400
☐ naive psychology	素朴心理学
☐ naive realism	素朴実在論
☐ naltrexone	ナルトレキソン
☐ nap; napping	昼寝
☐ narcissism	ナルシシズム，自己愛
☐ narcolepsy	ナルコレプシー
☐ narrative approach	ナラティブ・アプローチ
☐ narrative review	叙述的文献研究
☐ national character	国民性
☐ nativism	生得主義，生得説
☐ natural experiment	自然実験
☐ natural selection	自然選択，自然淘汰
☐ natural setting	自然場面
☐ natural stage	自然的段階
☐ naturalistic experiment	自然的実験
☐ naturalistic observation	自然(的)観察
☐ nature-nurture issue	遺伝・環境問題，氏か育ちか論争
☐ **need**	**欲求**，要求
☐ negative correlation	負の相関関係
☐ negative feedback	負のフィードバック
☐ negative hallucinations	陰性の幻覚
☐ negative punishment	負の罰
☐ negative reinforcement	負の強化
☐ negative transfer	負の転移
☐ neo-analytic theorist	新精神分析学派
☐ neo-Freudian	新フロイト派
☐ neobehaviorism	新行動主義
☐ neocortex	新皮質
☐ neonate	新生児
☐ neophobia	新奇性恐怖

☐ **nerve**	**神経**
☐ nerve conduction	神経伝導
☐ **nervous system**	**神経系**
☐ network model	ネットワーク・モデル
☐ neural network	神経網,ニューラル・ネットワーク
☐ neural sensitization	神経過敏性
☐ neuromodulator	神経修飾物質
☐ **neuron**	**神経細胞**,ニューロン
☐ neuronal model	神経モデル
☐ neurophysiology	神経生理学
☐ neuropsychology	神経心理学
☐ neurosis(複数:neuroses)	神経症
☐ neurotic anxiety	神経症的不安
☐ neuroticism	神経症的傾向
☐ neurotransmitter	神経伝達物質
☐ neutral density filter	NDフィルター
☐ **neutral stimulus, NS**	**中性刺激**
☐ node	節点,ノード
☐ noise	ノイズ,雑音
☐ nominal scale	名義尺度
☐ non-REM sleep, NREM sleep	ノンレム睡眠
☐ non-zero-sum game	非ゼロ和ゲーム
☐ nonassociative learning	非連合学習
☐ nondirective	非指示的
☐ nondirective counseling	非指示的カウンセリング
☐ nondirective interview	非指示的面接
☐ nonexperimental method	非実験法
☐ nonlinear	非線型
☐ nonliteral meaning	言外の意味
☐ nonparametric method	ノンパラメトリック法
☐ nonsense syllable	無意味綴り
☐ nonverbal behavior	非言語的行動
☐ nonverbal communication	非言語的コミュニケーション

☐ noradrenaline, NA	ノルアドレナリン
☐ norepinephrine, NE	ノルエピネフリン
☐ norm	規準，基準，規範
☐ norm group	基準集団，規範集団
☐ **normal distribution**	**正規分布**
☐ normality	正常，正規性
☐ normalization	ノーマライゼーション
☐ normative social influence	規範の社会的影響
☐ NS	⇨ neutral stimulus
☐ nuclear family	核家族
☐ nucleus	神経核
☐ **null hypothesis**	**帰無仮説**
☐ nystagmus	眼振

O

☐ obedience	服従
☐ obesity	肥満
☐ object permanence	対象の永続性，ものの永続性
☐ object relations theory	対象関係論
☐ objectification theory	対象化理論
☐ objective anxiety	現実不安
☐ objectivism	客観主義
☐ **observation**	**観察**
☐ observation method	観察法
☐ **observational learning**	**観察学習**
☐ observational study	観察的研究
☐ observed frequency	観測度数
☐ observer bias	観察者バイアス
☐ obsession	強迫観念
☐ obsessive-compulsive disorder	強迫症，強迫性障害
☐ obsessive-compulsive personality	強迫性パーソナリティ

☐ obstruction box	障害箱	
☐ occipital lobe	後頭葉	
☐ occupational therapist, OT	作業療法士	
☐ odds ratio	オッズ比	
☐ Oedipal conflict	エディプス葛藤	
☐ Oedipus complex	エディプス・コンプレックス	
☐ old-old	後期高齢者	
☐ olfaction	嗅覚	
☐ olfactory system	嗅覚系	
☐ omission training	省略訓練,オミッション訓練	
☐ one-tailed test	片側検定	
☐ one word sentence	一語文	
☐ ongoing EEG	通常脳波	
☐ ontogenetic development	個体発生的発達	
☐ ontogeny; ontogenesis	個体発生	
☐ open-ended question	自由回答法	
☐ openness	開放性	
☐ operant	オペラント	
☐ operant behavior	オペラント行動	
☐ **operant conditioning**	**オペラント条件づけ**	
☐ operant response	オペラント反応	
☐ operation	操作,手続き	
☐ operational definition	操作的定義	
☐ operationism	操作主義	
☐ operator	操作子	
☐ opiates	鎮痛薬	
☐ opponent-color theory	反対色説	
☐ opponent-process theory	相反過程説	
☐ optic nerve	視神経	
☐ optimism	楽観主義,オプティミズム	
☐ opto-electric method	光電子法	
☐ OR	⇨ orienting reflex	
☐ oral stage	口唇期	

☐ order effect	順序効果
☐ ordinal scale	順序尺度
☐ **organism**	**生活体**, 有機体
☐ organization	体制化, 組織
☐ organizational psychology	組織心理学
☐ orientation	定位
☐ **orienting reflex, OR**	**定位反射**
☐ orienting response, OR	定位反応
☐ originality	独創性
☐ orthogonal	直交
☐ oscillator	振動体, オシレータ
☐ out-group	外集団
☐ outcome evaluation	結果評価
☐ outcome expectancy	結果予期
☐ outer ear	外耳
☐ outer speech	外言
☐ outlier	外れ値
☐ overextension	過剰外延化
☐ overgeneralization	過剰般化
☐ overlearning	過剰学習
☐ **overt behavior**	**顕在行動**, あらわな行動
☐ oxygen consumption	酸素消費

P

☐ pain	痛覚, 痛み
☐ pair matching	対等化法
☐ paired associates method	対連合法
☐ paleocortex	古皮質
☐ pandemonium	パンデモニウム, 万魔殿
☐ panic	パニック
☐ panic attack	パニック発作
☐ panic disorder	パニック症[障害]

☐ paracontrast	パラコントラスト
☐ paradigm	パラダイム
☐ paragrammatism	錯文法
☐ parallel distributed processing model	並列分散処理モデル，PDPモデル
☐ parallel processing	並列処理
☐ parameter	母数，パラメータ
☐ parametric method	パラメトリック法
☐ paranoia	パラノイア
☐ paranoid	妄想型
☐ paraphrenia	パラフレニア
☐ parapsychology	超心理学
☐ **parasympathetic nervous system, PNS**	**副交感神経系**
☐ parietal lobe	頭頂葉
☐ Parkinson's disease	パーキンソン病
☐ parotid gland	耳下腺
☐ partial-report procedure	部分報告法
☐ **participant**	**参加者**
☐ participant modeling	参加型モデリング
☐ passion	情熱，熱情
☐ passionate love	情熱的な愛，熱愛
☐ passive attention	受動的注意
☐ pathology	病理(学)
☐ **patient**	**患者**
☐ pattern recognition	パターン認識
☐ Pavlovian conditioning	パブロフ型条件づけ
☐ pay-off matrix	利得行列
☐ peak experience	至高体験
☐ Pearson's product-moment correlation coefficient	ピアソンの積率相関係数
☐ pedagogy	教育学
☐ peer group	仲間集団
☐ percentile rank	パーセンタイル順位

☐ percentile score	パーセンタイル点	
☐ **perception**	**知覚**	
☐ perceptron	パーセプトロン	
☐ perceptual constancy	知覚の恒常性	
☐ perceptual defence	知覚的防衛	
☐ perceptual interference	知覚的干渉	
☐ perceptual learning	知覚学習	
☐ perceptual-motor learning	知覚運動学習	
☐ perceptual organization	知覚的体制化	
☐ perceptual set	知覚的構え	
☐ performance	パフォーマンス,遂行,作業,成績	
☐ performance test	作業検査法,動作性検査	
☐ period	周期	
☐ **peripheral nervous system**	**末梢神経系**	
☐ peripheral route	周辺経路	
☐ peripheral vision	周辺視	
☐ peripheralism	末梢主義	
☐ perseveration effect	固執効果	
☐ person centered therapy	人間中心療法	
☐ persona	ペルソナ,仮面	
☐ personal causality	個人的因果関係	
☐ personal construct	パーソナル・コンストラクト	
☐ personal space	パーソナル・スペース	
☐ **personality**	**パーソナリティ,人格**	
☐ personality disorder	パーソナリティ障害,人格障害	
☐ personality inventory	質問紙パーソナリティ検査,人格目録	
☐ personality psychology	パーソナリティ心理学,人格心理学	
☐ perspective	遠近,遠近法,展望	
☐ perspiration	発汗	
☐ persuasion	説得	
☐ pervasive developmental disorder	広汎性発達障害	

☐ **pessimism**	**悲観主義**, ペシミズム
☐ PET	⇨ positron emission tomography
☐ phallic stage	男根期
☐ phantom limb	幻肢
☐ phase	位相, 段階
☐ phase advance	位相前進
☐ phase delay	位相後退
☐ phase response	位相反応
☐ phase sequence	位相連鎖
☐ phasic arousal	一過性の覚醒
☐ phenomenology	現象学
☐ phenotype	表現型《生物の》
☐ pheromone	フェロモン
☐ phi-phenomenon	ファイ現象
☐ philosophy	哲学
☐ phobia	恐怖症
☐ phon	ホン
☐ phoneme	音素
☐ phonetic symbolism	音象徴
☐ phonological buffer	音韻的バッファー
☐ phonological code	音韻的符号
☐ phonological loop	音韻ループ
☐ photon	光子
☐ phrase	句
☐ phrase structure rule	句構造ルール
☐ phrenology	骨相学
☐ phylogeny; phylogenesis	系統発生
☐ physical attractiveness	身体的魅力
☐ physical description	物理的記述
☐ physical health	身体的な健康
☐ physical therapist, PT	理学療法士
☐ physics	物理学

☐ physiological premature delivery	生理的早産	
☐ **physiological psychology**	**生理心理学**	
☐ **physiology**	**生理学**	
☐ Pick's disease	ピック病	
☐ picture-frustration study, PF study	PFスタディ，絵画欲求不満テスト	
☐ pilot study	予備研究，パイロット・スタディ	
☐ pilot test	パイロット・テスト	
☐ pitch	音の高さ	
☐ **placebo**	**プラセボ**，プラシーボ，擬薬	
☐ placebo effect	プラセボ効果	
☐ plasticity	可塑性	
☐ plateau	プラトー現象，高原現象	
☐ play therapy	遊戯療法	
☐ pleasure principle	快楽原理	
☐ plethysmogram	容積脈派	
☐ pluralistic ignorance	多元的無知，多数の無知	
☐ point of subjective equality, PSE	主観的等価点	
☐ poll	世論調査	
☐ Pollyanna hypothesis	ポリアンナ仮説	
☐ polygraph	多種反応測定記録装置，ポリグラフ	
☐ POMS	⇨ Profile of Mood States	
☐ pons	橋	
☐ pop out	ポップアウト	
☐ **population**	**母集団**	
☐ positive correlation	正の相関関係	
☐ positive feedback	正のフィードバック	
☐ positive hallucination	陽性の幻覚	
☐ positive psychology	ポジティブ心理学	
☐ positive punishment	正の罰	
☐ positive reinforcement	正の強化	
☐ positive symptom	陽性症状	

☐ positive transfer	正の転移
☐ positivism	実証主義
☐ positron emission tomography, PET	陽電子放射断層撮影
☐ post hoc test	事後検定
☐ posthypnotic amnesia	後催眠健忘
☐ posthypnotic response	後催眠反応
☐ postmaterialist	脱物質主義
☐ posttest	事後テスト, ポストテスト
☐ **posttraumatic stress disorder, PTSD**	**心的外傷後ストレス障害**
☐ postulate	公準
☐ power function	ベキ関数
☐ power structure	勢力構造
☐ practice	実践, 慣用, 練習
☐ practice effect	練習効果
☐ pragma	プラグマ
☐ pragmatics	プラグマティクス, 語用論
☐ preattentive process	前注意過程
☐ precognitive emotion	前認知的感情
☐ preconsciousness	前意識
☐ precontemplation	無関心期
☐ predictability	予測可能性
☐ **prediction**	**予測**
☐ predictive validity	予測的妥当性
☐ predisposition	素因, 生得的傾向
☐ **preference**	**嗜好, 好み, 選好性**
☐ preference-looking technique	選好注視法
☐ prefrontal lobe	前頭前野
☐ prejudice	偏見
☐ Premack principle	プリマックの原理
☐ premature death	若年死
☐ prenatal period	出生前期

☐ preoccupation	先入観，先入見
☐ preoperational stage〔period〕	前操作段階〔期〕
☐ preparation	準備
☐ preparatory potential	準備電位
☐ preparatory response	準備反応
☐ preparedness	準備性
☐ pressure to uniformity	斉一性への圧力
☐ pretend play	ごっこ遊び
☐ preterm infant	早産児
☐ pretest	事前テスト，プリテスト，予備調査
☐ prevalence	有病率，流行，蔓延
☐ prevention	予防
☐ preventive health behavior	予防的健康行動
☐ primacy effect	初頭効果
☐ primary appraisal	一次的評価
☐ primary color	原色
☐ primary drive	一次的動因
☐ primary group	一次集団
☐ primary prevention	第一次予防
☐ primary reinforcer	一次強化子，一次性強化子
☐ prime	先行刺激，プライム
☐ **priming**	**プライミング**
☐ primitive feature	原始的特徴
☐ primitive stage	原始的段階
☐ principal component analysis	主成分分析
☐ principle	原理，原則
☐ prisoner's dilemma	囚人のジレンマ
☐ privacy	プライバシー
☐ proactive interaction	積極性相互作用，率先的相互作用
☐ proactive interference	順向干渉
☐ probable reasoning	蓋然性推理
☐ probe item	プローブ項目
☐ problem box	問題箱

☐ problem-focused coping	問題焦点型コーピング	
☐ **problem solving**	**問題解決**	
☐ problem-solving skill	問題解決スキル	
☐ problem space	問題空間	
☐ procedural knowledge	手続き的知識,手続き型知識	
☐ **procedural memory**	**手続き的記憶**,手続き型記憶	
☐ **procedure**	**手続き**	
☐ process evaluation	プロセス評価	
☐ processing capacity	処理容量	
☐ processing mode theory	処理様式説	
☐ processing negativity, PN	処理陰性電位	
☐ production	プロダクション,生産,産出	
☐ production deficiency	生産欠如	
☐ production of language	言語の産出	
☐ productive thinking	生産的思考	
☐ productivity	生産性	
☐ Profile of Mood States, POMS	気分プロフィール検査,感情プロフィール検査	
☐ programmed instruction	段階的教示	
☐ progressive muscle relaxation	漸進的筋弛緩法	
☐ projection	投射	
☐ projective technique	投影法,投映法	
☐ **projective test**	**投影検査**,投映検査	
☐ proposition	命題	
☐ propositional memory	命題記憶	
☐ propositional thought	命題的思考	
☐ proprioceptive sense	固有(受容性)感覚	
☐ prosocial behavior	向社会的行動	
☐ prosopagnosia	相貌失認	
☐ prospect theory	プロスペクト理論	
☐ prospective memory	展望的記憶	
☐ prospective study	前向き研究	
☐ protocol	プロトコル	

☐ prototype	原型，プロトタイプ	
☐ proximal stimulus	近接刺激	
☐ proximity	近接性，近接	
☐ PSE	⇨ point of subjective equality	
☐ pseudo-experiment	偽実験	
☐ psi	超常現象	
☐ psychiatrist	精神科医	
☐ **psychiatry**	**精神医学**	
☐ psychic	霊能力者，超能力者	
☐ psychic power	霊能力，超能力	
☐ psychic secretion	心的分泌，精神的分泌	
☐ psychoactive drug	精神活性薬	
☐ **psychoanalysis**	**精神分析(学)**	
☐ psychoanalytic theory	精神分析理論	
☐ psychodynamic therapy	精神力動的療法	
☐ **psychodynamics**	**精神力動，心理力動**	
☐ psychogenetic reaction	心因反応	
☐ psychograph	心誌	
☐ psycholinguistics	心理言語学	
☐ psychological determinism	心理学的決定論	
☐ psychological equivalence	心理的等価性	
☐ psychological satiation	心的飽和	
☐ Psychological Stress Response Scale, PSRS	心理的ストレス反応尺度	
☐ psychological test	心理検査，心理テスト	
☐ psychological variable	心理変数	
☐ psychologist	心理学者	
☐ **psychology**	**心理学**	
☐ psychometrics	計量心理学	
☐ psychoneuroimmunology	心理神経免疫学	
☐ psychopathology	精神病理学	
☐ psychopathy	精神病質	
☐ psychopharmacology	精神薬理学	

☐ psychophysical function	心理物理関数
☐ psychophysical isomorphism	心身同型説，心理物理同型説
☐ **psychophysics**	**精神物理学**，心理物理学
☐ psychophysiological disorder	心理生理的障害
☐ **psychophysiology**	**精神生理学**，心理生理学
☐ psychosexual stages	性心理的段階
☐ psychosis（複数：psychoses）	精神病
☐ psychosomatic	心身の
☐ psychosomatic disease; psychosomatic disorder	心身症
☐ psychosomatic medicine	心身医学
☐ **psychotherapy**	**心理療法**
☐ psychoticism	精神病的傾向
☐ PTSD	⇨ posttraumatic stress disorder
☐ puberty	思春期
☐ public health	公衆衛生
☐ pulse transit time, PTT	脈拍伝達〔播〕時間〔速度〕
☐ pulse wave	脈波
☐ **punishment**	**罰**
☐ pupil	瞳孔
☐ pupillary reflex	瞳孔反射
☐ pupillometry	瞳孔計
☐ purification	純化
☐ Purkinje phenomenon	プルキニエ現象
☐ purposive behavior	目的的行動
☐ puzzle box	問題箱
☐ Pygmalion effect	ピグマリオン効果

Q

☐ QOL	⇨ quality of life
☐ qualitative data	質的データ
☐ qualitative research method	質的研究法

☐ **qualitative variable**	**質的変数**
☐ quality	質
☐ quality of life, QOL	クオリティ・オブ・ライフ，生活の質
☐ quantification theory	数量化理論
☐ quantitative data	数量的データ
☐ **quantitative variable**	**量的変数**
☐ quasi-experiment	準実験
☐ **questionnaire**	**質問紙，調査票**
☐ questionnaire technique	質問紙法

R

☐ radical behaviorism	徹底的行動主義
☐ **random assignment**	**無作為割り当て，無作為配分**
☐ random dot stereogram, RDS	ランダムドット・ステレオグラム
☐ random effect	変量効果
☐ random error	偶然誤差
☐ random numbers	乱数
☐ random sample	無作為標本
☐ **random sampling**	**無作為抽出，ランダムサンプリング**
☐ randomization	無作為化
☐ randomized controlled trial, RCT	無作為化比較試験
☐ range	範囲
☐ rapid eye movement	急速眼球運動
☐ **rapid eye movement sleep, REM sleep**	**レム睡眠**
☐ **rapport**	**ラポール，親和的関係**
☐ rating scale	評定尺度
☐ ratio scale	比例尺度
☐ ratio schedule	比率スケジュール
☐ rational therapy	論理療法

☐ rational emotive behavior therapy, REBT	論理情動行動療法
☐ rationalization	合理化
☐ raw data	ローデータ，生のデータ
☐ raw score	素点，粗点
☐ reaching	リーチング，手のばし行動
☐ reactance	リアクタンス，変化への抵抗
☐ reaction formation	反動形成
☐ reaction potential	反応ポテンシャル
☐ **reaction time, RT**	**反応時間**
☐ reactive interaction	反応性相互作用
☐ reactivity	観察反応
☐ readiness	準備性，レディネス
☐ reality monitoring	リアリティ・モニタリング
☐ reality orientation, RO	リアリティ・オリエンテーション，現実見当識訓練
☐ reality principle	現実原理
☐ realness	真実性
☐ reasoning	推理
☐ rebound	跳ね返り
☐ REBT	⇨ rational emotive behavior therapy
☐ **recall**	**再生**
☐ receiver operant characteristic curve, ROC curve	受信者操作特性曲線《信号検出理論の》
☐ recency effect	新近性効果
☐ recentering	中心転換
☐ receptor	受容器，受容体，レセプター
☐ reciprocal inhibition	逆制止
☐ **recognition**	**再認**
☐ recognition memory	再認記憶
☐ recognition test	再認検査
☐ recognition threshold	認知閾
☐ reconstruction	再構成

☐ reductionism	還元主義
☐ **reference**	**引用文献**
☐ reference group	準拠集団
☐ reference memory	参照記憶
☐ referent power	準拠勢力
☐ reflectance characteristic	反射特徴
☐ reflection	反映,反射
☐ **reflex**	**反射**
☐ reflex arc	反射弓
☐ refractory period	不応期
☐ region of interest, ROI	関心領域
☐ region of rejection	棄却閾
☐ regression	退行,回帰
☐ regression analysis	回帰分析
☐ regular sleep	規則的睡眠
☐ **rehearsal**	**リハーサル**
☐ **reinforcement**	**強化**
☐ reinforcement theory	強化説
☐ reinforcer	強化子
☐ relative risk	相対リスク
☐ **relaxation**	**リラクセーション,弛緩**
☐ relaxation training	弛緩訓練
☐ releaser	触発子,解発子
☐ releasing stimulus	触発刺激,解発刺激
☐ **reliability**	**信頼性**
☐ REM cycle	レム周期
☐ REM sleep	⇨ rapid eye movement sleep
☐ reminiscence	レミニセンス,回想法
☐ reorganization	再体制化
☐ **replication**	**追試**,再現
☐ **representation**	**表象**
☐ representational mediation process	表象媒介過程

☐	representativeness heuristic	代表性ヒューリスティック
☐	repression	抑圧
☐	reproducibility	再現性
☐	reproductive memory	再生記憶
☐	reproductive thinking	再生的思考
☐	Rescorla-Wagner model	レスコーラ=ワグナー・モデル
☐	**research**	**研究**
☐	research hypothesis	研究仮説
☐	research paper	研究論文
☐	research presentation	研究発表
☐	researcher bias	研究者〔実験者〕バイアス
☐	residual	残差
☐	resilience	レジリエンス,回復力
☐	resistance	抵抗
☐	resonance	共鳴
☐	resource	資源
☐	resource-limited processing	資源依存型処理
☐	respiration	呼吸
☐	respondent	レスポンデント
☐	respondent conditioning	レスポンデント条件づけ
☐	**response**	**反応**,応答,回答
☐	response bias	反応バイアス
☐	response cost	反応コスト
☐	response latency	反応潜時
☐	response prevention	反応妨害法
☐	response time	反応時間
☐	resting membrane potential	静止膜電位
☐	restructuring	再構成
☐	**result**	**結果**
☐	retardation method	遅滞法
☐	retention	保持
☐	reticular formation	網様体
☐	retina	網膜

☐ retino-hypothalamic tract	網膜視床下部路
☐ **retrieval**	**検索**
☐ retrieval stage	検索段階
☐ retroactive interference	逆向干渉
☐ retrograde amnesias	逆向性健忘
☐ retrospective memory	回顧的記憶
☐ retrospective method	回想的方法
☐ retrospective study	後ろ向き研究
☐ reuptake	再取り込み
☐ reversal design	反転計画法
☐ **review**	**総説**, 展望, 査読
☐ **reward**	**報酬**, 賞
☐ reward conditioning	報酬性の条件づけ
☐ reward power	報酬勢力
☐ rhythm	リズム, 律動
☐ ribonucleic acid, RNA	リボ核酸
☐ right to privacy	プライバシーの権利
☐ rigidity	(人格的な)硬さ
☐ risk factor	危険因子, リスクファクター
☐ robustness	頑健性
☐ ROC curve	⇨ receiver operant characteristic curve
☐ rod	桿体
☐ **role**	**役割**
☐ role loss	役割喪失
☐ role playing	ロールプレイング
☐ role schema	役割スキーマ
☐ Rorschach Test	ロールシャッハ検査, ロールシャッハ・テスト
☐ routine EEG	通常脳波
☐ RT	⇨ reaction time
☐ rumor	流言, うわさ

S

☐ S	⇨ subject
☐ S factor	⇨ specific (intelligence) factor
☐ saccade	サッケイド,サッカード
☐ saccadic eye movement	サッカディック眼球運動
☐ saccadic suppression	サッカディック抑制
☐ saliency	顕著性
☐ saliva	唾液
☐ salivation	唾液分泌
☐ saltatory conduction	跳躍伝動
☐ **sample**	**標本**,サンプル
☐ sample survey	標本調査
☐ **sampling**	**標本抽出**,サンプリング
☐ sampling error	標本誤差,抽出誤差
☐ sandplay technique	箱庭療法
☐ Sapir-Whorf's hypothesis	サピア＝ウォーフの仮説
☐ SAT	⇨ Scholastic Assessment Test
☐ satiation	飽満
☐ satiety center	満腹中枢
☐ saturation	鮮やかさ,彩度,飽和
☐ **scale**	**尺度**,スケール
☐ scallop	スキャロップ現象
☐ scan	走査
☐ scatter diagram	散布図,相関図
☐ schedule of reinforcement	強化のスケジュール
☐ **schema**	**スキーマ**,シェマ,図式
☐ schematic processing	スキーマティック処理
☐ schizophrenia	統合失調症
☐ Scholastic Assessment Test, SAT	大学進学適性検査
☐ school counselor	学校カウンセラー
☐ school psychology	学校心理学
☐ school refusal	登校拒否,不登校

☐ Scientist-Practitioner Model	科学者-実践家モデル
☐ SCR	⇨ skin conductance response
☐ script	スクリプト
☐ SCT	⇨ sentence completion test
☐ SD	⇨ standard diviation
☐ searching reflex	探索反射，さがし反射
☐ second-order conditioning	二次条件づけ
☐ secondary appraisal	二次的評価
☐ secondary drive	二次的動因
☐ secondary group	二次集団
☐ secondary prevention	第二次予防
☐ secondary reinforcement	二次強化
☐ secondary reinforcer	二次性強化子
☐ secretion	分泌
☐ selective adaptation	選択的順応
☐ **selective attention**	**選択的注意**
☐ selective breeding	品種改良
☐ selective mutism	選択性緘黙，場面緘黙症
☐ selective reinforcement	選択的強化
☐ **self**	**自己**
☐ self-actualization	自己実現
☐ self-administration	自己投与
☐ self-care	セルフケア
☐ self-choice effect	自己選択効果
☐ self-concept	自己概念
☐ self-confidence	自信
☐ self-consciousness	自己意識，自意識
☐ self-control	自己制御
☐ self-disclosure	自己開示
☐ self-discrepancy theory	自己不一致理論
☐ self-efficacy	自己効力(感)
☐ self-enhancement	自己高揚
☐ **self-esteem**	**自尊心，自尊感情**

☐	self-expansion	自己拡張
☐	self-fulfilling prophecy	自己成就的予言
☐	self-generated elaboration	自己生成精緻化
☐	self-handicapping	セルフ・ハンディキャッピング
☐	self-help group	自助グループ
☐	self-instructional training	自己教示訓練
☐	self-management	セルフ・マネジメント,自己管理
☐	self-monitoring	セルフ・モニタリング,自己監視
☐	self-objectification	自己対象化
☐	self-perception theory	自己知覚理論
☐	self-presentation	自己呈示
☐	self-rating	自己評定
☐	self-reference effect	自己準拠効果,自己言及効果
☐	self-regulation	自己制御
☐	self-report	自己報告
☐	self-schema	自己スキーマ
☐	self-stimulation method	自己刺激法
☐	self-verification	自己確証
☐	SEM	⇨ standard error (of the mean)
☐	semantic code	意味的符号
☐	semantic differential method	セマンティック・ディファレンシャル法,SD法,意味微分法
☐	semantic feature theory	意味特徴仮説,意味的特徴説
☐	**semantic memory**	**意味記憶**
☐	semantic network	意味ネットワーク
☐	semi-structured interview	半構造化面接
☐	senescence	老年期
☐	**sensation**	**感覚**
☐	sensation level, SL	感覚レベル
☐	sense	感覚,気づき,良識
☐	sense organ	感覚器,感覚器官
☐	sensitive period	敏感期,鋭敏期
☐	sensitive responsiveness	応答感受性

☐ sensitivity	感受性, 感度	
☐ sensitization	鋭敏化, 感作	
☐ sensorimotor stage [period]	感覚運動段階[期]	
☐ sensory coding	感覚符号化	
☐ sensory deprivation	感覚遮断	
☐ sensory evaluation	官能検査, 感性評価	
☐ **sensory memory**	**感覚記憶**	
☐ sensory nerve	知覚[感覚]神経	
☐ sensory organ	感覚器官	
☐ sensory preconditioning	感性予備条件づけ	
☐ sensory register	感覚登録器	
☐ sensory response	感覚反応	
☐ sensory stimulus	感覚刺激	
☐ sensory storage	感覚貯蔵庫	
☐ sensory test	官能検査	
☐ sentence completion test, SCT	文章完成法	
☐ sentence verification task	文判断課題, 文の真偽判断課題	
☐ sentiment	情操, 情緒	
☐ separation anxiety	分離不安	
☐ serial position effect	系列位置効果	
☐ serial processing	直列型処理, 系列的処理	
☐ serial search	直列探索	
☐ serotonin	セロトニン	
☐ serotonin reuptake inhibitors	セロトニン再取り込み阻害薬	
☐ set	構え	
☐ set point	設定値	
☐ set-theoretic model	集合論モデル	
☐ sex	セックス, 性	
☐ sex role	性役割	
☐ sex typing	性の型づけ	
☐ sexual imprinting	性的刻印づけ, 性的刷り込み	
☐ sexual orientation	性的志向	
☐ sexual selection	性淘汰	

☐ sexual urge	性的衝動
☐ shading	陰影
☐ shadowing	追唱
☐ sham feeding	擬似給餌，にせの給餌
☐ shame	羞恥，恥
☐ **shaping**	**シェーピング，反応形成**
☐ **short-term memory, STM**	**短期記憶**
☐ short-term store, STS	短期貯蔵庫
☐ shuttle box	シャトル箱
☐ sick-role behavior	病者役割行動
☐ sign-Gestalt	サイン・ゲシュタルト
☐ sign tracking	サイントラッキング，信号追跡
☐ **signal**	**信号**
☐ signal detection theory, SDT	信号検出理論
☐ signal stimulus	信号刺激
☐ **significant**	**(統計的に)有意な，重要な**
☐ significant difference	有意差
☐ significant level	有意水準
☐ similarity	類同，類似(性)
☐ similarity heuristic	類似性ヒューリスティック
☐ simile	直喩
☐ simple cell	単純細胞
☐ simple phobia	単一恐怖
☐ simple reaction time, SRT	単純反応時間
☐ simulation	シミュレーション
☐ simultaneous conditioning	同時条件づけ
☐ single-blind test	単純盲検法
☐ single-case experiment	単一事例実験
☐ single-subject experiment	単一被験体研究，単一被験者研究
☐ situational attribution	状況帰属
☐ Sixteen PF test	16特性因子別性格検査
☐ size-distance invariance hypothesis	大きさ・距離関係不変仮説

☐ skill	技能，スキル
☐ skin conductance response, SCR	皮膚伝導反応
☐ skin-defense system	皮膚防衛システム
☐ skin potential response, SPR	皮膚電位反応
☐ skin resistance response, SRR	皮膚抵抗反応
☐ skin temperature	皮膚温
☐ Skinner box	スキナー・ボックス，スキナー箱
☐ **sleep**	**睡眠**
☐ sleep cycle	睡眠周期
☐ sleep disorder	睡眠障害
☐ sleep histogram	睡眠経過図
☐ sleep onset REM episode	入眠時レム
☐ sleep spindle	睡眠紡錘波
☐ sleep stage	睡眠段階
☐ sleep variable	睡眠変数
☐ slips of the tongue	言い間違い
☐ slow eye movement, SEM	緩徐眼球運動
☐ slow wave sleep, SWS	徐波睡眠
☐ smooth pursuit	追従眼球運動，追従運動
☐ Snellen acuity	スネレン視力
☐ social cognition	社会的認知
☐ social cognitive neuroscience	社会的認知神経科学
☐ social cognitive theory	社会的認知理論
☐ social comparison process	社会的比較過程
☐ social desirability	社会的望ましさ
☐ **social facilitation**	**社会的促進**
☐ social feeling	社会的感情
☐ social identity theory	社会的アイデンティティ理論
☐ social influence	社会的影響
☐ **social inhibition**	**社会的抑制**
☐ social isolation	社会的隔離
☐ social learning	社会的学習

☐ **social learning theory**	**社会的学習理論**	
☐ **social loafing**	**社会的手抜き**	
☐ social motive	社会的動機	
☐ social norm	社会規範	
☐ social penetration theory	社会的浸透理論	
☐ social perception	社会的知覚	
☐ social phobia	社交恐怖	
☐ social power	社会的勢力	
☐ **social psychology**	**社会心理学**	
☐ social readjustment rating scale, SRRS	社会的再適応評定尺度	
☐ social referencing	社会的参照	
☐ social schema	社会的スキーマ	
☐ **social skill**	**社会的スキル**, 社会的技能, ソーシャルスキル	
☐ social skills training, SST	社会(的)技能訓練, 社会的スキル訓練, ソーシャルスキルトレーニング	
☐ social stereotype	社会的ステレオタイプ	
☐ social support	ソーシャルサポート, 社会的支援	
☐ socialization	社会化	
☐ socioeconomic status, SES	社会経済的階級〔地位〕	
☐ sociogram	ソシオグラム	
☐ sociomatrix	ソシオマトリクス	
☐ sociometric structure	ソシオメトリック構造	
☐ sociometric test	ソシオメトリック・テスト	
☐ sociometry	ソシオメトリー	
☐ Solomon's design	ソロモン計画	
☐ somatic nervous system	体性神経系	
☐ somatosensory	体性感覚	
☐ sound pressure level, SPL	音圧レベル	
☐ sound wave	音波	
☐ source wavelengths	源波長	
☐ space perception	空間知覚	
☐ spaced learning	分散学習	

☐ span of apprehension	感知範囲
☐ spatial frequency	空間周波数
☐ species-specific defense reactions, SSDR	種に特有な防衛反応
☐ specific context effect	特定文脈効果
☐ specific hunger	特殊飢餓
☐ specific (intelligence) factor	特殊(知能)因子
☐ speech act	発話行為
☐ speech therapist, ST	言語聴覚士，スピーチセラピスト
☐ speed-accuracy trade-off	速度と正確さのトレードオフ
☐ spinal cord	脊髄
☐ spinal reflex	脊髄反射
☐ SPL	⇨ sound pressure level
☐ split brain	分離脳
☐ split-half reliability	折半法信頼性
☐ spontaneous blink	自発性瞬目
☐ spontaneous recovery	自発的回復，自然回復
☐ spreading activation model	活性化拡散モデル
☐ spurious correlation	擬似相関
☐ spurious noncorrelation	擬似無相関
☐ SST	⇨ social skills training
☐ stability	安定性
☐ stage of alarm reaction	警告反応期
☐ stage of change model	段階的変化モデル
☐ stage of exhaustion	疲憊期，疲弊期
☐ stage of resistance	抵抗期
☐ stages of development	発達段階
☐ STAI	⇨ State-Trait Anxiety Inventory
☐ staircase method	階段法
☐ standard	標準，基準
☐ **standard deviation, SD**	**標準偏差**
☐ standard error (of the mean), SEM	標準誤差

☐	standard score	標準得点
☐	**standardization**	**標準化**
☐	Stanford-Binet Intelligence Scale	スタンフォード・ビネー知能検査
☐	Stanford Sleepiness Scale, SSS	スタンフォード眠気尺度
☐	state dependency effect	状態依存効果
☐	state-dependent learning	状態依存学習
☐	State-Trait Anxiety Inventory, STAI	状態−特性不安尺度
☐	statistical model	統計モデル
☐	statistical power	検定力
☐	statistical significance	統計的有意性
☐	statistical test	統計的検定
☐	**statistics**	**統計学**
☐	status	地位
☐	steady state	定常状態, 安定状態
☐	stereotype	ステレオタイプ, 常同性
☐	Sternberg memory-scanning task	スタンバーグ記憶走査課題
☐	Stevens' law	スティーブンスの法則
☐	stimulants	興奮薬
☐	stimulation	刺激(作用)
☐	**stimulus**	**刺激**
☐	stimulus control	刺激性制御
☐	stimulus-driven processing	刺激駆動処理
☐	stimulus generalization	刺激般化
☐	stimulus-response, S-R	刺激-反応
☐	stimulus substitution	刺激置換
☐	stimulus threshold	刺激閾
☐	STM	⇨ short-term memory
☐	**storage**	**貯蔵**, ストレージ
☐	storage stage	貯蔵段階
☐	story grammar	物語文法
☐	straight alley	直線走路

☐ strange situation procedure	ストレンジ・シチュエーション法	
☐ strategy	方略	
☐ stratified sample	層別標本	
☐ **stress**	**ストレス**	
☐ **stress coping**	**ストレス対処**, ストレス・コーピング	
☐ stress management	ストレス・マネジメント	
☐ stress response	ストレス反応	
☐ **stressor**	**ストレッサー**	
☐ stroboscopic motion	ストロボスコープ運動, 驚盤運動	
☐ **Stroop effect**	**ストループ効果**	
☐ Stroop interference	ストループ干渉	
☐ structural equation modeling, SEM	構造方程式モデリング	
☐ **structuralism**	**構成主義**, 構造主義	
☐ structured interview	構造化面接	
☐ study of life history	ライフヒストリー研究	
☐ subconsciousness	下意識, 潜在意識	
☐ subculture	下位文化, サブカルチャー	
☐ **subject**	**被験者**, 被検者, 被験体	
☐ subject bias	被験者バイアス	
☐ subjective contour	主観的輪郭	
☐ subjective experience	主観的経験	
☐ subjective organization	主観的体制化	
☐ subjective well-being	主観的幸福感	
☐ sublimation	昇華	
☐ **subliminal perception**	**閾下知覚**	
☐ sublingual gland	舌下腺	
☐ submaxillary gland	顎下腺	
☐ subquestion	下位質問, サブクエスチョン	
☐ substance-related disorder	物質関連障害	
☐ substitute response	代償的反応	
☐ substitution theory	置換説	
☐ subtraction method	減算法	

☐ successful aging	サクセスフル・エイジング
☐ successive approximation	漸次的接近
☐ sucking reflex	吸啜反射，吸いつき反射
☐ suggestion	暗示
☐ suicide	自殺
☐ **summary**	**要約**
☐ summation method	加算法
☐ superego	超自我，スーパーエゴ
☐ supernormal stimulus	超正常刺激
☐ supervision	スーパーヴィジョン
☐ supervisor	スーパーヴァイザー
☐ suppression ratio, SR	抑制率
☐ suprachiasmatic nucleus, SCN	視交叉上核
☐ surface structure	表層構造
☐ surgency	高潮性
☐ **survey**	**調査**
☐ survey method	調査法
☐ survival	生存
☐ survival of the fittest	適者生存
☐ sustained channel	持続型(持続的)チャンネル
☐ switching	スイッチング
☐ symbol	象徴，シンボル
☐ symbolism	象徴主義，シンボリズム
☐ **sympathetic nervous system, SNS**	**交感神経系**
☐ symptom	症状，症候，徴候
☐ symptom substitute	代理症状
☐ **synapse**	**シナプス**
☐ synaptic plasticity	シナプス可塑性
☐ synchrony	同調傾向
☐ syndrome	症候群
☐ synecdoche	提喩
☐ synesthesia	共感覚

☐ syntax	統語
☐ system	システム
☐ systematic desensitization	系統的脱感作
☐ systematic error	系統誤差
☐ systric blood pressure, SBP	収縮期血圧

T

☐ T score	偏差値，T得点
☐ **t-test**	**t 検定**
☐ **table**	**表**
☐ tabula rasa	白紙状態，タブラ・ラサ
☐ tactile sensation	触覚
☐ talking cure	談話療法
☐ target	ターゲット，ターゲット項目，標的刺激
☐ target operant	標的オペラント
☐ taste aversion learning	味覚嫌悪学習
☐ taste receptor	味受容器
☐ TAT	⇨ Thematic Apperception Test
☐ taxis	走性
☐ teamwork	チームワーク
☐ telegraphic speech	電文体発話
☐ telepresence	テレプレゼンス
☐ **temperament**	**気質**
☐ template	鋳型
☐ temporal conditioning	時間条件づけ
☐ temporal-integration paradigm	時間的統合法
☐ temporal lobe	側頭葉
☐ temporal pattern	時間的様相
☐ temporal theory of sound	音の時間説
☐ tension	緊張

☐ terminal stimulus	刺激頂
☐ tertiary prevention	第三次予防
☐ **test**	**検査, テスト, 検定**
☐ test anxiety	テスト不安
☐ test battery	テスト・バッテリー
☐ test-retest reliability	再テスト法信頼性, 再検査信頼性
☐ texture gradient	きめの勾配
☐ thalamus	視床
☐ thanatology	死生学
☐ Thanatos	タナトス《死の本能》
☐ Thematic Apperception Test, TAT	主題統覚検査, 絵画統覚検査
☐ **theory**	**理論**
☐ **theory of evolution**	**進化論**
☐ theory of games	ゲーム理論
☐ theory of mind	心の理論
☐ **thinking**	**思考**
☐ thirst	渇き
☐ Thorndikean conditioning	ソーンダイク型条件づけ
☐ **thought**	**思考**
☐ thought and action tendencies	思考・行動傾向
☐ threat	脅威
☐ three-term contingency	三項随伴性
☐ **threshold**	**閾, 閾値**
☐ Thurstone scaling	サーストン尺度法
☐ tic	チック
☐ timbre	音色
☐ time out	タイムアウト
☐ time perception	時間知覚
☐ time variable	時間変数
☐ tip of the tongue phenomenon	のどまで出かかる現象, 舌端現象
☐ tit for tat strategy	しっぺ返し戦略
☐ **title**	**表題**

☐ token economy	トークン・エコノミー
☐ **tolerance**	**耐性**
☐ tonic arousal	持続性の覚醒
☐ top-down feedback connections	トップダウン・フィードバック結合
☐ **top-down processing**	**トップダウン処理**, 下降型処理
☐ topograph	トポグラフ
☐ tough-mindedness	タフ・マインド傾向
☐ trace conditioning	痕跡条件づけ
☐ tracking	追跡, トラッキング
☐ tragedy of the commons	共有地の悲劇, コモンズの悲劇
☐ **trait**	**特性**
☐ transaction	交流
☐ **transactional analysis**	**交流分析**
☐ transduction	変換
☐ transfer of control	コントロールの転移
☐ transfer of learning/training	学習／練習の転移
☐ transference	転移, 感情転移
☐ transformational generative grammar	変形生成文法
☐ transformational generative rule	変形生成規則
☐ transient channel	一過型〔一過性〕チャネル
☐ transitional object	移行対象
☐ transposition	移調
☐ transtheoretical model	汎理論的モデル
☐ **trauma**	**心的外傷**, トラウマ, 外傷
☐ traumatic event	外傷的出来事
☐ **treatment**	**治療**, 処遇, 処置
☐ tree drawing test	樹木画テスト, バウムテスト
☐ tremor	ふるえ, 振せん
☐ **trial**	**試行**
☐ trial-and-error	試行錯誤
☐ trial-by-trial analysis	試行ごとの分析

☐ triangular theory of love	恋愛の三要素説
☐ triarchic theory of intelligence	知能の三部理論
☐ trichromatic theory	三色説
☐ tricyclic antidepressant	三環系抗うつ薬
☐ truly random control, TRC	真にランダムな統制条件
☐ two-factor theory	二要因理論
☐ two-process theory of learning	学習の二過程説
☐ two-tailed test	両側検定
☐ **type**	**類型**
☐ Type A behavior	タイプA行動
☐ type I error	第1種の誤り〔過誤〕
☐ type II error	第2種の誤り〔過誤〕
☐ typology	類似論
☐ typicality	典型性

U

☐ UCR	⇨ unconditioned response, UR
☐ UCS	⇨ unconditioned stimulus, US
☐ ultradian rhythm	ウルトラディアン・リズム，縮日周期
☐ unconditional positive regard	無条件の肯定的配慮
☐ **unconditioned reflex**	**無条件反射**
☐ **unconditioned response, UR; UCR**	**無条件反応**
☐ **unconditioned stimulus, US; UCS**	**無条件刺激**
☐ **unconsciousness**	**無意識**
☐ undirected thinking	目標づけられない思考
☐ undoing	打ち消し
☐ uniformity	斉一性
☐ universality	普遍性
☐ unlearned behavior	非学習性の行動
☐ unrealistic optimism	非現実的楽観主義

unstructured interview	非構造化面接
UR	⇨ unconditioned response, UCR
US	⇨ unconditioned stimulus, UCS

V

valence	誘意性, 価
validation	妥当性検証, 妥当化
validity	**妥当性**
value	値, 価値, 明度
variable	**変数**
variable interval schedule	変(動)間隔スケジュール
variable ratio schedule	変(動)比率スケジュール
variance	**分散**
variance analysis	分散分析
ventromedial hypothalamus	視床下部の腹内側核《飽食中枢》
verbal behavior	言語行動
verbal label	言語ラベル
verbal measure	言語測度
verbal mediating response	言語媒介反応
verbal test	言語性検査
vergence movement	輻輳開散運動
verification	検証
vertical axis	縦軸
vertical eye movement	垂直眼球運動
vicarious conditioning	代理条件づけ
vicarious learning	代理学習
vicarious reinforcement	代理強化
vigilance	ヴィジランス
visceral perception	内臓知覚
visceral response	内臓反応
visible spectrum	可視スペクトル
vision	**視覚**

☐ visual acuity	視力
☐ visual cliff	視覚的断崖
☐ visual code	視覚的符号
☐ visual cortex	視覚野
☐ visual field	視野
☐ visual illusion	錯視
☐ visual image	視覚イメージ，視覚心像
☐ visual information storage, VIS	視覚情報保持
☐ visual masking	視覚マスキング
☐ visual neglect	視覚的無視
☐ visual perception	視知覚
☐ visual search	視覚探索
☐ visual-spatial sketchpad	視空間スケッチパッド
☐ Vocational Preference Inventory	VPI 職業興味検査
☐ voluntary	随意(の)，自発性(の)
☐ voluntary activity	随意活動
☐ voluntary behavior	随意行動
☐ voluntary blink	随意性瞬目
☐ voluntary control	随意制御
☐ voluntary movement	随意運動
☐ voluntary response	随意反応
☐ vulnerability-stress model	ストレス脆弱性モデル

W

☐ WAIS	⇨ Wechsler Adult Intelligence Scale
☐ waking activity	活動的覚醒
☐ weapon focus effect	凶器注目効果
☐ Weber fraction	ウェーバー比
☐ Weber's law	ウェーバーの法則

☐ Wechsler Adult Intelligence Scale, WAIS	ウェクスラー成人知能検査
☐ Wechsler Intelligence Scale for Children, WISC	ウェクスラー児童用知能検査
☐ Wechsler Memory Scale, WMS	ウェクスラー記憶検査
☐ well-being	安寧，幸福，ウェルビーイング
☐ well-established treatment	効果が十分証明された治療
☐ Wernicke's aphasia	ウェルニッケ失語症
☐ Wernicke's area	ウェルニッケ野《＝感覚性言語中枢》
☐ what-is-it reflex	おやなんだ反応
☐ white matter	白質
☐ white noise	白色ノイズ，ホワイトノイズ
☐ whole-report condition	全体報告条件
☐ will	意志
☐ WISC	⇨ Wechsler Intelligence Scale for Children
☐ wisdom	知恵
☐ withdrawal	退避，離脱，ひきこもり
☐ withdrawal symptoms	離脱症状，禁断症状
☐ within-individual variation	個体内変動
☐ **within-subject(s) design**	**被験者内計画**
☐ within-subject(s) factor	被験者内要因
☐ wording	ワーディング
☐ working backwards	逆向き解決法
☐ **working memory**	**作業記憶，作動記憶，ワーキングメモリー**

Y

☐ Yerkes-Dodson law	ヤーキーズ=ダッドソンの法則
☐ yoked control technique	連動統制法
☐ young-old	前期高齢者

Z

- [ ] z score — 標準得点, z得点
- [ ] zero-sum game — ゼロ和ゲーム
- [ ] zone of proximal development — 発達の最近接領域

ギリシャ

- [ ] α attenuation — アルファ減衰
- [ ] α wave — アルファ波
- [ ] β wave — ベータ波
- [ ] δ wave — デルタ波
- [ ] θ wave — シータ波

あ 行

☐ 愛《キリスト教的な》	agape
☐ アイコニックメモリー	iconic memory
☐ アイコンタクト	eye contact
☐ 愛情	love
☐ 愛他行動	altruistic behavior
☐ 愛他性	altruism
☐ **愛着**	**attachment**
☐ アイデンティティ	identity
☐ アイデンティティ拡散	identity diffusion
☐ アガペー	agape
☐ 明るさ	brightness
☐ アーキタイプ	archetype
☐ アサーション・トレーニング	assertion training
☐ 鮮やかさ	saturation
☐ アセスメント	assessment
☐ アソシエーション	association
☐ 値	value
☐ アドレナリン	adrenaline
☐ アナログ表象	analogical representation
☐ アニミズム	animism
☐ アパシー	apathy
☐ アハ体験	aha experience
☐ アフォーダンス	affordance
☐ アメリカ心理学会	American Psychological Association, APA
☐ アメリカ精神医学会	American Psychiatric Association, APA
☐ あらわでない行動	covert behavior
☐ あらわな行動	overt behavior
☐ アルゴリズム	algorithm
☐ アルコール中毒(症)〔依存(症)〕	alcoholism
☐ アルツハイマー病	Alzheimer's disease

☐ アルファ〔α〕係数	coefficient alpha
☐ アルファ減衰	α attenuation
☐ アルファ波	α wave
☐ アレキシサイミア	alexithymia
☐ 暗示	suggestion
☐ 暗順応	dark adaptation
☐ 暗順応曲線	dark adaptation curve
☐ 安定状態	steady state
☐ 安定性	stability
☐ 安寧	well-being
☐ アンビバレンス	ambivalence
☐ アンフェタミン	amphetamine
☐ 言い間違い	slips of the tongue
☐ 胃運動性	gastric motility
☐ イオンチャネル	ion channel
☐ 医学〔疾病〕モデル	medical〔disease〕model
☐ 鋳型	template
☐ **怒り**	**anger**
☐ 怒りの制御	anger control
☐ 怒りの表出	anger out
☐ 怒りの抑制	anger in
☐ **閾,閾値**	**threshold**; limen
☐ **閾下知覚**	**subliminal perception**
☐ 育児語	motherese
☐ 移行対象	tramsitional object
☐ 意志	will
☐ 維持	maintenance
☐ **意識**	**consciousness**
☐ **意識性**	**awareness**
☐ 意思決定	decision making
☐ **異常**	**abnormal**
☐ 異常行動	abnormal behavior
☐ 維持リハーサル	maintenance rehearsal

☐ 位相	phase
☐ 位相後退	phase delay
☐ 位相前進	phase advance
☐ 位相反応	phase response
☐ 位相連鎖	phase sequence
☐ 依存症, 依存性	dependency
☐ 痛み	pain
☐ 痛みの関門制御〔ゲートコントロール〕理論	gate control theory of pain
☐ 一語文	one word sentence
☐ 一次(性)強化子	primary reinforcer
☐ 一次集団	primary group
☐ 一次的動因	primary drive
☐ 一次的評価	primary appraisal
☐ 移調	transposition
☐ 一卵性双生児	identical twins; monozygotic twins
☐ 一過型〔一過性〕チャネル	transient channel
☐ 一過性の覚醒	phasic arousal
☐ 一貫性	consistency
☐ 一色型色覚	monochromatism
☐ 逸脱	drift
☐ 逸脱行動	deviant behavior
☐ (自己)一致	congruence
☐ 一致係数	coefficient of concordance
☐ 一致的妥当性	consensual validation
☐ 一対比較法	method of paired comparisons
☐ 一般化	generalization
☐ 一般遅延モデル	general slowing model
☐ 一般(知能)因子	general (intelligence) factor; g factor
☐ 一般適応症候群	general adaptive syndrome, GAS
☐ 一般的文脈効果	general context effect
☐ イデオロギー	ideology

☐ 遺伝	heredity
☐ 遺伝・環境問題	nature-nurture issue
☐ 遺伝規定性	heritability
☐ 遺伝形質〔特性〕	inherited characteristics
☐ **遺伝子**	**gene**
☐ 遺伝子型	genotype
☐ 遺伝子多型	genetic polymorphism
☐ 遺伝的要因	genetic factor
☐ 意図	intention
☐ **イド《エスと同じ》**	**id**
☐ 意図的処理〔過程〕	control process
☐ 異文化間	cross-cultural
☐ 異文化間心理学	cross-cultural psychology
☐ 意味	meaning
☐ **意味記憶**	**semantic memory**
☐ 意味的符号	semantic code
☐ 意味特徴(仮)説	semantic feature theory
☐ 意味ネットワーク	semantic network
☐ 意味微分法	semantic differential method
☐ イメージ	image; imagery
☐ イメージ的思考	imaginal thought
☐ 色の恒常性	color constancy
☐ 陰影	shading
☐ **因果関係**	**causal relationship; causality**
☐ 因果性ヒューリスティック	causality heuristic
☐ 因果法則，因果律	law of causality
☐ インクのしみ，インクブロット	inkblot
☐ **因子**	**factor**
☐ **因子分析**	**factor analysis**
☐ **印象**	**impression**
☐ 印象形成	impression formation
☐ 印象操作	impression management
☐ インストラクション	instruction

☐ 陰性の幻覚	negative hallucinations
☐ インテーク面接	intake interview
☐ インパクト評価	impact evaluation
☐ インパルス	impulse
☐ インフォーマル	informal
☐ インフォーマルグループ	informal group
☐ **インフォームド・コンセント**	**informed consent**
☐ インフラディアン・リズム	infradian rhythm
☐ インプリンティング	imprinting
☐ 隠喩	metaphor
☐ **引用文献**	**reference**
☐ ヴィジランス	vigilance
☐ 飢え	hunger
☐ ウェクスラー記憶検査	Wechsler Memory Scale, WMS
☐ ウェクスラー児童用知能検査	Wechsler Intelligence Scale for Children, WISC
☐ ウェクスラー成人知能検査	Wechsler Adult Intelligence Scale, WAIS
☐ ウェーバー比	Weber fraction
☐ ウェーバーの法則	Weber's law
☐ ウェルニッケ失語症	Wernicke's aphasia
☐ ウェルニッケ野《感覚性言語中枢》	Wernicke's area
☐ ウェルビーイング	well-being
☐ 氏か育ちか論争	nature-nurture issue
☐ 後ろ向き研究	retrospective study
☐ **嘘発見**	**lie detection**
☐ 嘘発見器	lie detector
☐ 打ち消し	undoing
☐ **うつ病**	**depression**
☐ うつ病性障害	depressive disorder
☐ ウルトラディアン・リズム	ultradian rhythm
☐ うわさ	rumor
☐ **運動**	**movement**

☐ 運動感覚	kinesthesis
☐ 運動視差	motion parallax
☐ 運動障害	dyskinesia
☐ 運動神経	motor nerve
☐ 運動性言語中枢	Broca's area
☐ 運動性構音障害	dysarthria
☐ 運動単位	motor unit
☐ 運動電位	motor potential
☐ 運動皮質	motor cortex
☐ 栄光浴	basking in reflected glory
☐ エイジング	aging
☐ ABAB計画法	ABAB design
☐ 鋭敏化	sensitization
☐ 鋭敏期	sensitive period
☐ 疫学	epidemiology
☐ エゴ	ego
☐ エコイックメモリー	echoic memory
☐ エス《イドと同じ》	es
☐ SD法	semantic differential method
☐ エディプス葛藤	Oedipal conflict
☐ エディプス・コンプレックス	Oedipus complex
☐ N2-P3複合	N2-P3 complex
☐ NDフィルター	neutral density filter
☐ エピソード	episode
☐ **エピソード記憶**	**episodic memory**
☐ エピネフリン《＝アドレナリン》	epinephrine
☐ FFT法	fast Fourier transform
☐ ML法	maximum likelihood method, MLM
☐ エルゴノミクス	ergonomics
☐ エレクトラ・コンプレックス	Electra complex
☐ エロス	Eros
☐ **演繹**	**deduction**

☐ 演繹的推論	deductive inference
☐ エンカウンター・グループ	encounter group
☐ 遠隔刺激	distal stimulus
☐ 婉曲表現	euphemism
☐ 遠近(法)	perspective
☐ 演色性	color rendering property
☐ 援助行動	helping behavior
☐ 遠心性神経	efferent nerve
☐ 遠心的	centrifugal
☐ 延髄	medulla
☐ 延滞条件づけ	delay conditioning
☐ 応諾	compliance
☐ 横断研究	cross-sectional research; cross-sectional study
☐ 応答	response
☐ 応答感受性	sensitive responsiveness
☐ **応用行動分析**	**applied behavior analysis**
☐ 応用心理学	applied psychology
☐ 大きさ・距離関係不変仮説	size-distance invariance hypothesis
☐ 置き換え	displacement
☐ 奥行知覚	depth perception
☐ 奥行き手がかり	depth cue
☐ オシレータ	oscillator
☐ **恐れ**	**fear**
☐ オッズ比	odds ratio
☐ オートシェイピング	autoshaping
☐ 音象徴	phonetic symbolism
☐ 音の大きさ	loudness
☐ 音の時間説	temporal theory of sound
☐ 音の高さ	pitch
☐ オプティミズム	optimism
☐ オペラント	operant

☐ オペラント行動	operant behavior
■ **オペラント条件づけ**	**operant conditioning**
☐ オペラント反応	operant response
☐ オミッション訓練	omission training
☐ おやなんだ反応	what-is-it reflex
☐ 音圧レベル	sound pressure level, SPL
☐ 音韻的バッファー	phonological buffer
☐ 音韻的符号	phonological code
☐ 音韻ループ	phonological loop
☐ 音楽療法	music therapy
☐ 音響記憶	echoic memory
☐ 音素	phoneme
☐ 音波	sound wave

か　行

☐ 価	valence
☐ 外因性電位	exogenous potentials
☐ 外延的意味	denotative meaning
☐ 絵画統覚検査	Thematic Apperception Test, TAT
☐ 絵画欲求不満テスト	picture-frustration study, PF study
☐ 回帰	regression
☐ 回帰分析	regression analysis
☐ 外言	outer speech
☐ 外向型	extrovert
■ **外向性**	**extraversion; extroversion**
☐ 回顧的記憶	retrospective memory
☐ 外耳	outer ear
☐ 下意識	subconsciousness
☐ 下位次元	facet
☐ 下位質問	subquestion
☐ 概日リズム	circadian rhythm

☐ 解釈	interpretation
☐ 外集団	out-group
☐ 回収率	completion rate
☐ 外傷	trauma
☐ 外傷後ストレス障害	posttraumatic stress disorder, PTSD
☐ 外傷的出来事	traumatic event
☐ 蓋然性推理	probable reasoning
☐ 階層的ネットワーク・モデル	hierarchical network model
☐ 回想的方法	retrospective method
☐ 回想法	reminiscence
☐ 外側視床下部《摂食中枢》	lateral hypothalamus
☐ 外側膝状体	lateral geniculate body, LGB
☐ 階段法	staircase method
☐ 外的妥当性	external validity
☐ 外的統制	external control
☐ 回答	response
☐ 解読	decoding
☐ **カイ二乗検定**	**chi square test**
☐ 介入	interpositon
☐ 介入研究	intervention study
☐ **概念**	**concept**
☐ 概念化	conceptualization
☐ 概念駆動型処理	conceptually driven processing
☐ 概念形成	concept formation
☐ 概念作用	conception
☐ 概念的表象	conceptual representation
☐ 海馬	hippocampus
☐ 灰白質	gray(grey) matter
☐ 解発子	releaser
☐ 解発刺激	releasing stimulus
☐ 外罰的反応	extrapunitive response
☐ **回避**	**avoidance**

☐ 回避－回避葛藤	avoidance-avoidance conflict
☐ 回避学習	avoidance learning
☐ 回復力	resilience
☐ 下位文化	subculture
☐ 開放性	openness
☐ 快楽原理	pleasure principle
☐ 快楽喪失	anhedonia
☐ 解離	dissociation
☐ 解離性症〔障害〕	dissociative disorder
☐ 解離性同一性症〔障害〕	dissociative identity disorder
☐ **カウンセリング**	**counseling**
☐ **カウンターバランス**	**counterbalance**
☐ 化学	chemistry
☐ 科学者－実践家モデル	Scientist-Practitioner Model
☐ 蝸牛	cochlea
☐ 核家族	nuclear family
☐ 拡散的思考	divergent thinking
☐ 核磁気共鳴画像診断	magnetic resonance imaging, MRI
☐ **学習**	**learning**
☐ 学習曲線	learning curve
☐ **学習症〔障害〕**	**learning disability; learning disorder, LD**
☐ **学習性(の)無力感，学習性絶望**	**learned helplessness**
☐ 学習の構え，学習セット	learning set
☐ 学習の生物的制約	biological constraints on learning
☐ 学習の二過程説	two-process theory of learning
☐ 学習／練習の転移	transfer of learning/training
☐ 確証バイアス	confirmation bias
☐ **覚醒**	**arousal**
☐ 覚醒水準	arousal level
☐ 覚醒理論	arousal theory
☐ 拡張期血圧	diastolic blood pressure, DBP
☐ カクテルパーティ効果	cocktail party effect

☐ 獲得	acquisition
☐ 確認的因子分析	confirmatory factor analysis, CFA
☐ かく乱	distraction
☐ 隔離	isolation
☐ 隠れた観察者	hidden observer
☐ 仮現運動	apparent movement
☐ 下降型処理	top-down processing
☐ 下降系列	descending series
☐ 下降試行	descending trial
☐ 重なり《奥行き知覚の》	interposition
☐ 加算法	summation method
☐ 加算誘発電位	averaged EP, AEP
☐ 加算要因法	additive factor method
☐ 可視運動	apparent movement
☐ 可視スペクトル	visible spectrum
☐ 過剰外延化	overextension
☐ 過剰学習	overlearning
☐ 過剰般化	overgeneralization
☐ **仮説**	**hypothesis**（複数：**hypotheses**）
☐ 仮説演繹法	hypothetico-deductive method
☐ 仮説検証	hypothesis verification
☐ 仮説的構成概念	hypothetical construct
☐ 画像記憶	iconic memory
☐ 家族療法	family therapy
☐ 可塑性	plasticity
☐ 片側検定	one-tailed test
☐（人格的な）硬さ	rigidity
☐ 偏り	bias
☐ 偏りのある標本	biased sample
☐ カタルシス	catharsis
☐ カタルシス法	cathartic method
☐ 価値	value
☐ 顎下腺	submaxillary gland

☐	学校カウンセラー	school counselor
☐	学校心理学	school psychology
☐	活性化拡散モデル	spreading activation model
☐	**葛藤**	**conflict**
☐	**活動,活動性**	**activity**
☐	活動的覚醒	waking activity
☐	活動電位	action potential
☐	カップル療法	couple therapy
☐	カテゴリー	category
☐	カテゴリー化	categorization
☐	カテコールアミン	catecholamine
☐	ガードナー多重知能理論	Gardner's theory of multiple intelligence
☐	カバー・ストーリー	cover story
☐	構え	set
☐	仮面	persona
☐	加齢	aging
☐	渇き	thirst
☐	環	link
☐	**感覚**	**sensation; sense**
☐	感覚運動段階〔期〕	sensorimotor stage〔period〕
☐	感覚器	sense organ
☐	**感覚記憶**	**sensory memory**
☐	感覚器官	sense organ; sensory organ
☐	感覚刺激	sensory stimulus
☐	間隔尺度	interval scale
☐	感覚遮断	sensory deprivation
☐	間隔スケジュール	interval schedule
☐	感覚性言語中枢	Wernicke's area
☐	感覚貯蔵庫	sensory storage
☐	感覚登録器	sensory register
☐	感覚反応	sensory response
☐	感覚符号化	sensory coding

☐ 感覚誘発電位	evoked potential, EP
☐ 感覚様相	modality
☐ 感覚レベル	sensation level, SL
☐ 喚起	arousal
☐ 喚起性相互作用	evocative interaction
☐ **眼球運動**	**eye movement**
☐ 眼球停留	fixation pause
☐ 眼球停留関連電位	eye fixation-related potential
☐ **環境**	**environment**
☐ 環境主義	environmentalism
☐ 環境変数	environmental variable
☐ 間欠強化	intermittent reinforcement
☐ 還元主義	reductionism
☐ 頑健性	robustness
☐ 眼瞼反射	eyelid reflex
☐ 感作	sensitization
☐ **観察**	**observation**
☐ **観察学習**	**observational learning**
☐ 観察者間信頼性	interobserver reliability
☐ 観察者バイアス	observer bias
☐ 観察的研究	observational study
☐ 観察反応	reactivity
☐ 観察法	observation method
☐ **患者**	**patient**
☐ 感受性	sensitivity
☐ **干渉**	**interference**
☐ **感情**	**feeling; affect; emotion**
☐ 感情価	hedonic value
☐ 干渉説	interference theory
☐ 感情調整	emotion regulation
☐ 感情転移	transference
☐ 冠状動脈性心臓疾患	coronary heart disease, CHD
☐ 感情プロフィール検査	Profile of Mood States, POMS

☐ 干渉変数	interfering variable
☐ 緩徐眼球運動	slow eye movement, SEM
☐ 関心	contemplation
☐ 関心領域	region of interest, ROI
☐ 眼振	nystagmus
☐ 関数	function
☐ 感性評価	sensory evaluation
☐ 感性予備条件づけ	sensory preconditioning
☐ 観測度数	observed frequency
☐ 桿体	rod
☐ 感知範囲	span of apprehension
☐ ガンツフェルト法	ganzfeld procedure
☐ 眼電図	electrooculogram, EOG
☐ 感度	sensitivity
☐ 観念運動	ideomotor action
☐ 間脳	diencephalon
☐ 官能検査	sensory evaluation; sensory test
☐ 顔面フィードバック仮説	facial feedback hypothesis
☐ 緘黙	mutism
☐ 換喩	metonymy
☐ 関与	engagement
☐ 慣用	practice
☐ 完了的行動	consummatory behavior
☐ **記憶**	**memory**
☐ 記憶痕跡	memory trace
☐ 記憶術	mnemonics
☐ 記憶の障害	amnesia
☐ 記憶範囲	memory span
☐ 記憶負荷	memory load
☐ 記憶方略	memory strategy
☐ 飢餓	hunger
☐ 飢餓感固有の痛み	hunger pang
☐ 機械論	mechanism

☐ 危機	crisis
☐ 棄却閾	region of rejection
☐ 危急反応	emergency reaction
☐ 危険因子	risk factor
☐ 擬似給餌	sham feeding
☐ 擬似相関	spurious correlation
☐ **気質**	**temperament**; disposition
☐ 偽実験	pseudo-experiment
☐ 擬似無相関	spurious noncorrelation
☐ **記述統計(量), 記述統計学**	**descriptive statistics**
☐ 規準	norm
☐ 基準	norm; standard
☐ 基準関連妥当性	criterion related validity
☐ 基準集団	norm group
☐ 基準妥当性	criterion validity
☐ 基準比率の誤り	base rate fallacy
☐ 基準変数	criterion variable
☐ **帰属**	**attribution**
☐ 帰属過程	attribution process
☐ 規則的睡眠	regular sleep
☐ 帰属様式	attributional style
☐ 帰属理論	attribution theory
☐ 基礎水準	basic level
☐ **期待**	**expectation**
☐ 期待度数	expected frequency
☐ 既知感	feeling of knowing
☐ 気づき	awareness; sense
☐ 拮抗条件づけ	counterconditioning
☐ 拮抗薬	antagonist
☐ 基底膜	basilar membrane
☐ 輝度	luminance
☐ 機能	function
☐ **帰納**	**induction**

☐ 技能	skill
☐ 機能局在	functional localization
☐ **機能主義**	**functionalism**
☐ 帰納推理	inductive reasoning
☐ 機能的固着,機能的固定	functional fixedness
☐ 機能的磁気共鳴画像	functional magnetic resonance imaging, fMRI
☐ 機能的自律性	functional autonomy
☐ 機能的非対称性	functional asymmetry
☐ 機能特殊化説	functional specialization theory
☐ 機能不全	dysfunction
☐ 規範	norm
☐ 規範集団	norm group
☐ 規範の社会的影響	normative social influence
☐ ギフテッド	gifted
☐ **気分**	**mood**
☐ 気分一致効果	mood congruency effect
☐ 気分障害	mood disorder
☐ 気分状態依存効果	mood state dependency effect
☐ 気分プロフィール検査	Profile of Mood States, POMS
☐ 基本的動機	basic motive
☐ 基本的な帰属の誤り	fundamental attribution error
☐ **帰無仮説**	**null hypothesis**
☐ 記銘	memorization
☐ きめの勾配	texture gradient
☐ きめの細かさ	grain size
☐ 擬薬	placebo
☐ 逆制止	reciprocal inhibition
☐ **虐待**	**abuse**
☐ 逆転移	countertransference
☐ 逆向き解決法	working backwards
☐ 客観主義	objectivism
☐ 逆向干渉	retroactive interference

☐ 逆行条件づけ	backward conditioning
☐ 逆向性健忘	retrograde amnesias
☐ 逆行性投射	back projections
☐ 逆行性マスキング	backward masking
☐ **キャノン゠バード説**	**Cannon-Bard theory**
☐ キャリーオーバー効果	carryover effect
☐ ギャングエイジ	gang age
☐ ギャンブラーの誤謬〔錯誤〕	gambler's fallacy
☐ 求援助行動	help seeking behavior
☐ 嗅覚	olfaction
☐ 嗅覚系	olfactory system
☐ 給仕装置への馴致訓練	magazine training
☐ 求心性神経	afferent nerve
☐ 求心的	centripetal
☐ 急性ストレス障害	acute stress disorder
☐ 急速眼球運動	rapid eye movement
☐ 吸啜反射	sucking reflex
☐ 橋	pons
☐ 脅威	threat
☐ 教育学	pedagogy
☐ 教育心理学	educational psychology
☐ 教育老年学	educational gerontology
☐ 鏡映描写	mirror drawing
☐ **強化**	**reinforcement**
☐ 境界性パーソナリティ障害	borderline personality disorder
☐ 強化子	reinforcer
☐ 強化説	reinforcement theory
☐ 強化のスケジュール	schedule of reinforcement
☐ 共感(性)	empathy
☐ 共感覚	synesthesia
☐ 凶器注目効果	weapon focus effect
☐ 共行動	coaction
☐ 共行動集団	coacting group

☐ 教示	**instruction**
☐ 凝視	fixation; gaze
☐ 胸式呼吸	chest breathing
☐ 凝集性	cohesiveness
☐ 強靭さ	hardiness
☐ 強制勢力	coersive power
☐ 強制選択法	forced-choice method
☐ 共通性	communality
☐ **強度**	**intensity**
☐ 強迫観念	obsession
☐ 強迫	compulsion
☐ 強迫症, 強迫性障害	obsessive-compulsive disorder
☐ 強迫性パーソナリティ	obsessive-compulsive personality
☐ 驚盤運動	stroboscopic motion
☐ **恐怖**	**fear**
☐ 恐怖症	phobia
☐ 恐怖条件づけ	fear conditioning
☐ 共分散	covariance
☐ 共分散構造分析	covariance structure analysis, CSA
☐ 共分散分析	analysis of covariance, ANCOVA
☐ 共変原理	covariation principle
☐ 共変数	covariate
☐ 共鳴	resonance
☐ 共有地の悲劇	tragedy of the commons
☐ 虚偽記憶	false memory
☐ 虚偽教示	deception
☐ 虚偽検出	detection of deception
☐ 極限法	method of limits
☐ 虚再認	false recognition
☐ 寄与リスク	attributable risk
☐ 議論	discussion
☐ 筋, 筋肉	muscle
☐ 均衡状態	balance

□ 均衡理論	equilibrium theory
□ 近接，近接性	proximity
□ 近接刺激	proximal stimulus
□ 近接による群化	grouping by proximity
□ 禁断症状	withdrawal symptoms
□ 緊張	tension
□ 筋電位	muscle potential
□ 筋電図	electromyogram, EMG
□ 勤勉性	conscienciousness
□ 句	phrase
□ 空間周波数	spatial frequency
□ 空間知覚	space perception
□ 偶然誤差	random error
□ 空想	fantasy
□ 偶発学習	incidental learning
□ クオリティ・オブ・ライフ	quality of life, QOL
□ 区間推定(法)	interval estimation
□ 句構造ルール	phrase structure rule
□ 具体的操作段階〔期〕	concrete operational stage〔period〕
□ 苦痛	distress
□ クライエント	client
□ **クライエント中心療法**	**client centered therapy**
□ クラスター分析	cluster analysis
□ グリア細胞	glia cells
□ グループ	group
□ グループダイナミックス	group dynamics
□ クロス集計	cross tabulation
□ **群**	**group**
□ 群衆	crowd
□ 経験主義	empiricism
□ 経験的妥当性	criterion validity
□ 迎合行動	ingratiation
□ 警告反応期	stage of alarm reaction

☐ 形式	formal
☐ 形式的操作段階〔期〕	formal operational stage〔period〕
☐ 芸術療法	art therapy
☐ 傾(向)性	disposition
☐ 形態心理学	Gestalt psychology
☐ 形態素	morpheme
☐ 系統誤差	systematic error
☐ 系統的脱感作	systematic desensitization
☐ 系統発生	phylogeny; phylogenesis
☐ 形容詞チェックリスト	adjective check list, ACL
☐ 係留効果	anchoring effect
☐ 計量心理学	psychometrics
☐ 系列位置効果	serial position effect
☐ 系列的処理	serial processing
☐ ゲシュタルト	Gestalt
☑ **ゲシュタルト心理学**	**Gestalt psychology**
☐ ゲシュタルト療法	Gestalt therapy
☐ ケース構築, ケースフォーミュレーション	case formulation
☐ ゲセルシャフト	gesellschaft
☐ 血圧	blood pressure, BP
☑ **結果**	**result**; consequence
☐ 結果の知識	knowledge of result, KR
☐ 結果評価	outcome evaluation
☐ 結果予期	outcome expectancy
☐ 結合	connection
☐ 結合(の)問題	binding problem
☐ 結晶性知能	crystallized intelligence
☐ 血流	blood flow
☐ 血量	blood volume
☐ ゲマインシャフト	gemeinschaft
☐ ゲーム理論	theory of games
☐ 権威	authority

□ 権威主義的パーソナリティ	authoritarian personality
□ 原因帰属	causal attribution
□ 嫌悪条件づけ	aversive conditioning
□ 嫌悪療法	aversion therapy
□ 言外の意味	nonliteral meaning
□ **幻覚**	**hallucination**
□ 幻覚薬	hallucinogen
□ **研究**	**research**
□ 研究仮説	research hypothesis
□ 研究者〔実験者〕バイアス	researcher bias
□ 研究発表	research presentation
□ 研究論文	research paper
□ 元型	archetype
□ 原型	prototype
□ 言語	language
□ 健康科学	health sciences
□ 健康関連行動	health-related behavior
□ 健康行動	health behavior
□ 健康習慣	health practices
□ 健康主義	healthism
□ 健康信念モデル	health belief model
□ 健康心理学	health psychology
□ 言語学	linguistics
□ (生得的)言語獲得装置	language acquisition device
□ 言語行動	verbal behavior
□ 言語習得装置	linguistic acquisition device
□ 言語症〔障害〕	language disorder
□ 言語性検査	verbal test
□ 言語相対性仮説	linguistic relativity hypothesis
□ 言語測度	verbal measure
□ 言語聴覚士	speech therapist, ST
□ 言語の産出	production of language
□ 言語媒介反応	verbal mediating response

☐ 言語普遍性	linguistic universal
☐ 言語ラベル	verbal label
☐ **検査**	**test**
☐ 顕在記憶	explicit memory
☐ **顕在行動**	**overt behavior**
☐ 顕在性不安尺度	Manifest Anxiety Scale, MAS
☐ 顕在内容	manifest content
☐ **検索**	**retrieval**
☐ 検索段階	retrieval stage
☐ 検査作業	inspection task
☐ 減算法	subtraction method
☐ 幻肢	phantom limb
☐ 現実見当識訓練	reality orientation , RO
☐ 現実原理	reality principle
☐ 現実暴露法	in vivo exposure
☐ 現実否認	denial
☐ 現実不安	objective anxiety
☐ 原始的段階	primitive stage
☐ 原始的特徴	primitive feature
☐ 検証	verification
☐ 現象学	phenomenology
☐ 原色	primary color
☐ 減衰説	decay theory
☐ 原則	principle
☐ 顕著性	saliency
☐ 検定	test
☐ 検定力	statistical power
☐ 現場実験	field experiment
☐ 源波長	source wavelengths
☐ 原皮質	archicortex
☐ 健忘(症)	amnesia
☐ 原理	principle
☐ 語彙判断課題	lexical decision task

☐ 好意	liking
☐ 行為者-観察者バイアス	actor-observer bias
☐ 行為障害	conduct disorder
☐ 合意性	consensus
☐ 抗うつ薬	antidepressant
☐ 効果が十分証明された治療	well-established treatment
☐ 効果器	effector
☐ 工学心理学	engineering psychology
☐ 効果の法則	law of effect
☐ 効果量	effect size
☐ **交感神経系**	**sympathetic nervous system, SNS**
☐ 後期高齢者	old-old
☐ 好奇心	curiosity
☐ 後期陽性成分	late positive component, LPC
☐ 攻撃行動	aggressive behavior
☐ **攻撃性**	**aggression**
☐ 後件	consequent
☐ 高原現象	plateau
☐ **交互作用**	**interaction**
☐ 交互作用効果	interaction effect
☐ 虹彩	iris
☐ 後催眠健忘	posthypnotic amnesia
☐ 後催眠反応	posthypnotic response
☐ **考察**	**discussion**
☐ 光子	photon
☐ 公式	formal
☐ 公式集団	formal group
☐ 公式な規範	formal norm
☐ 高次条件づけ	higher-order conditioning
☐ 向社会的行動	prosocial behavior
☐ 公衆衛生	public health
☐ 公準	postulate
☐ 恒常条件	constant condition

☐ **恒常性**	**constancy; homeostasis**
☐ 恒常的動作パターン	fixed action pattern, FAP
☐ 恒常法	constant method
☐ 口唇期	oral stage
☐ 構成概念	construct
☐ 構成概念妥当性	construct validity
☐ **構成主義**, 構造主義	**structuralism**
☐ 構成的過程	constructive process
☐ 構成的知覚	constructive perception
☐ 構造化面接	structured interview
☐ 構造方程式モデリング	structural equation modeling, SEM
☐ 高速フーリエ変換	fast Fourier transform, FFT
☐ 高潮性	surgency
☐ 光電子法	opto-electric method
☐ **行動**	**behavior**
☐ 行動アセスメント	behavior assessment
☐ 行動医学	behavioral medicine
☐ 行動遺伝学	behavior genetics; behavioral genetics
☐ 行動科学	behavioral science
☐ 行動観察	behavioral observation
☐ 行動経済学	behavioral economics
☐ 行動修正	behavior modification
☐ **行動主義**	**behaviorism**
☐ 行動主義者	behaviorist
☐ 行動障害	behavior disorder
☐ 行動生態学	behavioral ecology
☐ 行動生物学	ethology
☐ 行動生物学者	ethologist
☐ 行動測度	behavioral measure
☐ 行動評価	behavioral assessment
☐ **行動分析**	**behavior analysis**
☐ **行動変容**	**behavior modification**

☐ 後頭葉	occipital lobe
☐ 行動リスク要因	behavioral risk factors
☐ 行動リハーサル	behavior rehearsal
☐ **行動療法**	**behavior therapy**; behavioral therapy
☐ 光背効果	halo-effect
☐ 広汎性発達障害	pervasive developmental disorder
☐ 幸福	well-being
☐ 興奮	excitement; excitation
☐ 興奮条件づけ	excitatory conditioning
☐ 興奮性結合	excitatory connections
☐ 興奮薬	stimulants
☐ 公平〔衡平〕理論	equity theory
☐ 項目応答理論	item response theory, IRT
☐ 項目特性曲線	item characteristic curve
☐ 項目反応理論	item response theory, IRT
☐ 項目分析	item analysis
☐ 肛門期	anal stage
☐ 交絡感作	cross sensitization
☐ 交絡する	confound
☐ 交絡抵抗	crossed resistance
☐ 交絡変数	confounding variable
☐ 合理化	rationalization
☐ 交流	transaction
☐ **交流分析**	**transactional analysis**
☐ 効力予測	efficacy expectancy
☐ コーエンのカッパ係数	Cohen's κ coefficient
☐ 誤帰属	misattribution
☐ 呼吸	respiration
☐ **刻印づけ**	**imprinting**
☐ 国民性	national character
☐ 心の理論	theory of mind
☐ **誤差**	**error**

用語(和→英) こう〜こさ

☐ 誤差逆伝播学習則	error back propagation learning rule
☐ 固視	fixation
☐ 固視点	fixation point
☐ 固執効果	perseveration effect
☐ **個人差**	**individual difference**
☐ 個人主義	individualism
☐ 個人的因果関係	personal causality
☐ 個性	individuality
☐ 個性化	individualization; individuation
☐ 個体化	individuation
☐ **個体差**	**individual difference**
☐ 個体内変動	individuality; within-individual variation
☐ 個体発生	ontogeny; ontogenesis
☐ 個体発生的発達	ontogenetic development
☐ 固着	fixation
☐ ごっこ遊び	pretend play
☐ 骨相学	phrenology
☐ 固定間隔スケジュール	fixed interval schedule
☐ 固定効果	fixed effect
☐ 固定比率スケジュール	fixed ratio schedule
☐ **古典的条件づけ**	**classical conditioning**
☐ 孤独感	aloneness
☐ コネクショニスト・ネットワーク	connectionist network
☐ コネクショニスト・モデル	connectionist model
☐ コーネル大学健康調査票	Cornell Medical Index, CMI
☐ 子の刻印づけ，子の刷り込み	filial imprinting
☐ 好み	preference
☐ 古皮質	paleocortex
☐ **コーピング**	**coping**
☐ 個別化	individuation
☐ 誤報《信号検出理論の》	false alarm, FA

☐ コーホート分析	cohort analysis
☐ 鼓膜	eardrum
☐ コミットメント	commitment
☐ **コミュニケーション**	**communication**
☐ コミュニケーション・ネットワーク	communication network
☐ コミュニティ	community
☐ コモンズの悲劇	tragedy of the commons
☐ 固有(受容性)感覚	proprioceptive sense
☐ 語用論	pragmatics
☐ ゴルジ染色	Golgi's method
☐ コルチコイド	corticoid
☐ コルチコステロイド	corticosteroid
☐ コルチゾール	cortisol
☐ コレクト・リジェクション《信号検出理論の》	correct rejection
☐ **根拠**	**evidence**; ground
☐ 痕跡条件づけ	trace conditioning
☐ コンテクスト	context
☐ コントロールの転移	transfer of control
☐ コンピタンス	competence
☐ コンピューター学習	computer assisted learning, CAL
☐ コンピューター支援教育	computer assisted instruction, CAI
☐ コンピューター・シミュレーション	computer simulation
☐ コンピューター断層撮影	computer tomography, CT
☐ コンプライアンス	compliance
☐ コンフリクト	conflict
☐ コンプレックス	complex

さ 行

☐ 再現	replication

☐ 再検査信頼性	test-retest reliability
☐ 再現性	reproducibility
☐ 再構成	reconstruction; restructuring
☐ **再生**	**recall**
☐ 再生記憶	reproductive memory
☐ 再生的思考	reproductive thinking
☐ 最大エントロピー法	maximum entropy method, MEM
☐ 再体制化	reorganization
☐ 差異的確率の原理	differential probability principle
☐ 再テスト法信頼性	test-retest reliability
☐ 彩度	chroma; saturation
☐ 再取り込み	reuptake
☐ **再認**	**recognition**
☐ 再認記憶	recognition memory
☐ 再認検査	recognition test
☐ サイバネティックス	cybernetics
☐ **最頻値**	**mode**
☐ 細胞集成体	cell assembly
☐ **催眠**	**hypnosis**
☐ 催眠暗示	hypnotic suggestion
☐ 最尤法	maximum likelihood method, MLM
☐ (実験)材料	material
☐ サイン・ゲシュタルト	sign-Gestalt
☐ サイントラッキング	sign tracking
☐ さがし反射	searching reflex
☐ サーカディアン・リズム	circadian rhythm
☐ 作業	performance
☐ **作業記憶**	**working memory**
☐ 作業検査法	performance test
☐ 作業療法士	occupational therapist, OT
☐ 錯誤帰属	misattribution
☐ 錯視	visual illusion
☐ サクセスフル・エイジング	successful aging

☐ 錯文法	paragrammatism
☐ サクラ	confederate
☐ サーストン尺度法	Thurstone scaling
☐ 雑音	noise
☐ **錯覚**	**illusion**
☐ 錯覚的結合	illusory conjunction
☐ サッカディック眼球運動	saccadic eye movement
☐ サッカディック抑制	saccadic suppression
☐ サッケイド, サッカード	saccade
☐ **査定**	**assessment**
☐ 作動記憶	working memory
☐ 査読	review
☐ サピア゠ウォーフの仮説	Sapir-Whorf's hypothesis
☐ サブカルチャー	subculture
☐ サブクエスチョン	subquestion
☐ 作用心理学	act psychology
☐ 作用薬	agonist
☐ 参加型モデリング	participant modeling
☐ **参加者**	**participant**
☐ 三環系抗うつ薬	tricyclic antidepressant
☐ 産業心理学	industrial psychology
☐ 残効	after effect
☐ 三項随伴性	three-term contingency
☐ 残差	residual
☐ 産出	production
☐ 参照記憶	reference memory
☐ 三色説	trichromatic theory
☐ 残像	after image
☐ 酸素消費	oxygen consumption
☐ 散布図	scatter diagram
☐ サンプリング	sampling
☐ サンプル	sample
☐ 算法	algorithm

☐ 残留効果	carryover effect
☐ 死	death
☐ 地	ground
☐ 自意識	self-consciousness
☐ 恣意性	arbitrary
☐ **シェーピング**	**shaping**
☐ シェマ	schema
☐ **ジェームズ゠ランゲ説**	**James-Lange theory**
☐ **ジェンダー**	**gender**
☐ ジェンダー・スキーマ	gender schema
☐ **自我**	**ego**
☐ **視覚**	**vision**
☐ 視覚イメージ	visual image
☐ 視覚情報保持	visual information storage, VIS
☐ 視覚心像	visual image
☐ 視覚探索	visual search
☐ 視覚的断崖	visual cliff
☐ 視覚的符号	visual code
☐ 視覚的無視	visual neglect
☐ 視覚マスキング	visual masking
☐ 視覚野	visual cortex
☐ 耳下腺	parotid gland
☐ **自我同一性**	**identity**
☐ 自我同一性の拡散	identity diffusion
☐ **弛緩**	**relaxation**
☐ 弛緩訓練	relaxation training
☐ 時間条件づけ	temporal conditioning
☐ 時間知覚	time perception
☐ 時間的統合法	temporal-integration paradigm
☐ 時間的様相	temporal pattern
☐ 時間変数	time variable
☐ 士気	morale

☐ 磁気共鳴画像，磁気共鳴断層撮影	magnetic resonance imaging, MRI
☐ 色相	hue
☐ 磁気誘発電位	magneto-evoked potential
☐ 視空間スケッチパッド	visual-spatial sketchpad
☐ 軸索	axon
☐ **刺激**	**stimulus**
☐ 刺激(作用)	stimulation
☐ 刺激閾	stimulus threshold
☐ 刺激間間隔	interstimulus interval, ISI
☐ 刺激駆動処理	stimulus-driven processing
☐ 刺激性制御	stimulus control
☐ 刺激置換	stimulus substitution
☐ 刺激頂	terminal stimulus
☐ 刺激般化	stimulus generalization
☐ 刺激-反応	stimulus-response, S-R
☐ 資源	resource
☐ 次元	dimension; domain
☐ 資源依存型処理	resource-limited processing
☐ 試験管内測定	in vitro measurement
☐ **自己**	**self**
☐ 自己愛	narcissism
☐ 自己意識	self-consciousness
☐ **思考**	**thinking; thought**
☐ **試行**	**trial**
☐ **嗜好**	**preference**
☐ 試行(間)間隔	intertrial interval, ITI
☐ 思考・行動傾向	thought and action tendencies
☐ 試行ごとの分析	trial-by-trial analysis
☐ 試行錯誤	trial-and-error
☐ 視交叉上核	suprachiasmatic nucleus, SCN
☐ 志向性	intentionality
☐ 至高体験	peak experience

☐ 自己開示	self-disclosure
☐ 自己概念	self-concept
☐ 自己確証	self-verification
☐ 自己拡張	self-expansion
☐ 自己監視	self-monitoring
☐ 自己管理	self-management
☐ 自己教示訓練	self-instructional training
☐ 自己言及効果	self-reference effect
☐ 事後検定	post hoc test
☐ 自己高揚	self-enhancement
☐ 自己効力(感)	self-efficacy
☐ 自己刺激法	self-stimulation method
☐ 自己実現	self-actualization
☐ 自己充足的コミュニケーション	consumatory communication
☐ 自己主張	assertion
☐ 自己主張訓練	assertion training
☐ 自己準拠効果	self-reference effect
☐ 自己成就的予言	self-fulfilling prophecy
☐ 自己スキーマ	self-schema
☐ 自己制御	self-control; self-regulation
☐ 自己生成精緻化	self-generated elaboration
☐ 事後説明	debriefing
☐ 自己選択効果	self-choice effect
☐ 自己対象化	self-objectification
☐ 自己知覚理論	self-perception theory
☐ 自己中心語	egocentric speech
☐ 自己中心性	egocentrism
☐ 自己中心的思考	egocentric thinking
☐ 自己中心的発話	egocentric speech
☐ 自己呈示	self-presentation
☐ 事後テスト	posttest
☐ 自己投与	self-administration

☐ 自己評定	self-rating
☐ 自己不一致理論	self-discrepancy theory
☐ 自己報告	self-report
☐ 自殺	suicide
☐ 指示的意味	denotative meaning; extensional meaning
☐ 思春期	puberty
☐ 視床	thalamus
☐ 視床下部	hypothalamus
☐ 視床下部の腹内側核《飽食中枢》	ventromedial hypothalamus
☐ **事象関連(脳)電位**	**event-related (brain) potential, ERP**
☐ 事象スキーマ	event schema
☐ 自助グループ	self-help group
☐ 自信	self-confidence
☐ 視神経	optic nerve
☐ システム	system
☐ 死生学	thanatology
☐ 指先〔尖〕温	finger temperature
☐ 自然回復	spontaneous recovery
☐ 自然(的)観察	naturalistic observation
☐ 自然実験	natural experiment
☐ 自然選択	natural selection
☐ 自然的実験	naturalistic experiment
☐ 自然的段階	natural stage
☐ 事前テスト	pretest
☐ 自然淘汰	natural selection
☐ 自然場面	natural setting
☐ 持続型(持続的)チャンネル	sustained channel
☐ 持続性の覚醒	tonic arousal
☐ **自尊心, 自尊感情**	**self-esteem**
☐ シータ波	θ wave
☐ 視知覚	visual perception

☐ 質	quality
☐ 失音楽症	amusia
☐ 失感情症	alexithymia
☐ **実験**	**experiment**
☐ 実験観察法	experimental observation
☐ 実験協力者	confederate
☐ **実験群**	**experimental group**
☐ 実験計画	experimental design
☐ 実験室実験	laboratory experiment
☐ **実験者**	**experimenter**
☐ 実験者効果	experimenter effect
☐ 実験条件	experimental condition
☐ **実験心理学**	**experimental psychology**
☐ 実験制御	experimental control
☐ 実験的行動分析	experimental analysis of behavior
☐ 実験的統制	experimental control
☐ 実験法	experimental method
☐ 実行可能性	feasibility
☐ 失語症	aphasia
☐ 実証主義	positivism
☐ 実証的研究	empirical study
☐ 実践	practice
☐ 実存分析	logotherapy
☐ 実存療法	existential therapy
☐ 質的研究法	qualitative research method
☐ 質的データ	qualitative data
☐ **質的変数**	**qualitative variable**
☐ 失認	agnosia
☐ 失文法	agrammatism
☐ 疾病モデル	disease model
☐ しっぺ返し戦略	tit for tat strategy
☐ 失名辞失語症	anomic aphasia
☐ 失名詞症	anomic aphasia

☐ **質問紙**	**questionnaire**; inventory
☐ 質問紙パーソナリティ検査	personality inventory
☐ 質問紙法	questionnaire technique
☐ 自伝的記憶	autobiographical memory
☐ 自動運動	autokinetic
☐ **児童期**	**childhood**
☐ 児童虐待	child abuse
☐ 自動形成	autoshaping
☐ 自動思考	autonomic thoughts
☐ 自動性	automaticity
☐ 自動的処理〔過程〕	automatic process
☐ **シナプス**	**synapse**
☐ シナプス可塑性	synaptic plasticity
☐ 自発性(の)	voluntary
☐ 自発性瞬目	spontaneous blink
☐ 自発的回復	spontaneous recovery
☐ 自分らしさ	authenticity
☐ **自閉症**	**autism**
☐ 自閉スペクトラム症	autism spectrum disorder, ASD
☐ 自閉性障害	autistic disorder
☐ 嗜癖	addiction
☐ 死への準備教育	death education
☐ シミュレーション	simulation
☐ 自民族中心主義	ethnocentrism
☐ 視野	visual field
☐ 社会化	socialization
☐ 社会(的)技能訓練	social skills training, SST
☐ 社会規範	social norm
☐ 社会〔社交〕恐怖	social phobia
☐ 社会経済的階級〔地位〕	socioeconomic status, SES
☐ **社会心理学**	**social psychology**
☐ 社会的アイデンティティ理論	social identity theory
☐ 社会的影響	social influence

☐ 社会的隔離	social isolation
☐ 社会的学習	social learning
☐ **社会的学習理論**	**social learning theory**
☐ 社会的感情	social feeling
☐ 社会的技能	social skill
☐ 社会的再適応評定尺度	social readjustment rating scale, SRRS
☐ 社会的参照	social referencing
☐ 社会的支援	social support
☐ 社会的浸透理論	social penetration theory
☐ 社会的スキーマ	social schema
☐ **社会的スキル**	**social skill**
☐ 社会的スキル訓練	social skills training, SST
☐ 社会的ステレオタイプ	social stereotype
☐ 社会的知覚	social perception
☐ 社会的勢力	social power
☐ **社会的促進**	**social facilitation**
☐ **社会的手抜き**	**social loafing**
☐ 社会的動機	social motive
☐ 社会的認知	social cognition
☐ 社会的認知神経科学	social cognitive neuroscience
☐ 社会的認知理論	social cognitive theory
☐ 社会的望ましさ	social desirability
☐ 社会的比較過程	social comparison process
☐ **社会的抑制**	**social inhibition**
☐ **尺度**	**scale**
☐ 若年死	premature death
☐ シャトル箱	shuttle box
☐ 自由オペラント	free operant
☐ 重回帰分析	multiple regression analysis
☐ 自由回答法	open-ended question
☐ 習慣	habit
☐ 習慣強度	habit strength

□ 周期	period
□ 自由継続リズム	free-running rhythm
□ 集合的無意識	collective unconscious
□ 集合論モデル	set-theoretic model
□ 自由再生	free recall
□ 収縮	contraction
□ 収縮期血圧	systric blood pressure, SBP
□ 囚人のジレンマ	prisoner's dilemma
□ 収束的思考	convergent thinking
□ 収束的妥当性	convergent validity
□ **従属変数**	**dependent variable**
□ **集団**	**group**
□ 集団圧力	group pressure
□ 集団規範	group norm
□ 集団凝集性	group cohesiveness
□ 集団極性化効果	group polarization effect
□ **縦断研究**	**longitudinal study**; longitudinal research
□ 集団思考	groupthink
□ 集団実験	group experiment
□ 集団主義	collectivism
□ 集団目標	collective goal
□ 集団力学	group dynamics
□ 集団療法	group therapy
□ 羞恥	shame
□ **自由度**	**degree of freedom**
□ 習得	acquisition
□ 周波数	frequency
□ 自由反応	free response
□ 周辺経路	peripheral route
□ 周辺視	peripheral vision
□ 重要な	significant
□ 自由連想(法)	free association

☐ 16特性因子別性格検査	Sixteen PF test
☐ 主観的経験	subjective experience
☐ 主観的幸福感	subjective well-being
☐ 主観的体制化	subjective organization
☐ 主観的等価点	point of subjective equality, PSE
☐ 主観的輪郭	subjective contour
☐ 縮日周期	ultradian rhythm
☐ 熟達(化)	expertize
☐ 熟知度	familiarity
☐ 主効果	main effect
☐ 樹状突起	dendrite
☐ 受信者操作特性曲線《信号検出理論の》	receiver operant characteristic curve, ROC curve
☐ 主成分分析	principal component analysis
☐ 主題統覚検査	Thematic Apperception Test, TAT
☐ 手段としての攻撃性	instrumental aggression
☐ 手段・目標分析	means-ends analysis
☐ 出生前期	prenatal period
☐ 受動的注意	passive attention
☐ 種に特有な防衛反応	species-specific defense reactions, SSDR
☐ 守秘義務	confidentiality
☐ 樹木画テスト	tree drawing test; Baumtest
☐ 受容	acceptance
☐ 受容器	receptor
☐ (性格の)主要5因子	Big Five
☐ 受容体	receptor
☐ 受理面接	intake interview
☐ 純化	purification
☐ **馴化**	**habituation**
☐ 馴化効果	habituation effect
☐ 馴化・脱馴化法	habituation-dishabituation technique

☐ 馴化法	habituation method
☐ 準拠集団	reference group
☐ 準拠勢力	referent power
☐ 準拠枠	frame of reference
☐ 順向干渉	proactive interference
☐ 順向性マスキング	forward masking
☐ 準実験	quasi-experiment
☐ 順序効果	order effect
☐ 順序尺度	ordinal scale
☐ 純粋性	genuineness
☐ **順応**	**adaptation**
☐ 準備	preparation
☐ 準備性	preparedness; readiness
☐ 準備電位	preparatory potential
☐ 準備反応	preparatory response
☐ **瞬目**	**blink**; eyeblink
☐ 瞬目反射	blink reflex
☐ 賞	reward
☐ 上位・下位分析	good-poor analysis; G-P analysis
☐ 昇華	sublimation
☐ 消化	digestion
☐ 浄化	catharsis
☐ 障害箱	obstruction box
☐ 生涯発達	lifespan development
☐ 生涯有病率	lifetime prevalence rate
☐ **消去**	**extinction**
☐ 状況帰属	situational attribution
☐ **条件刺激**	**conditioned stimulus, CS**
☐ 条件性強化子	conditioned reinforcer
☐ 条件性嫌悪	conditioned aversion
☐ 条件性満腹感	conditioned satiety
☐ 条件性抑制	conditioned suppression
☐ 条件即応理論	contingency theory

☐ **条件づけ**	**conditioning**
☐ 条件づけられた	conditioned
☐ **条件反射**	**conditioned reflex**
☐ **条件反応**	**conditioned response, CR**
☐ 証拠	evidence
☐ 症候	symptom
☐ 症候群	syndrome
☐ 常識心理学	common sense psychology
☐ 症状	symptom
☐ 上昇型処理	bottom-up processing
☐ 上昇系列〔試行〕	ascending series〔trial〕
☐ 少数者集団	minority
☐ 少数の法則	law of small numbers
☐ 少数派の影響	minority influence
☐ 情操	sentiment
☐ 状態依存学習	state-dependent learning
☐ 状態依存効果	state dependency effect
☐ 状態−特性不安尺度	State-Trait Anxiety Inventory, STAI
☐ 承諾先取り法, 承諾先取要請法	low-ball technique
☐ 情緒	emotion; sentiment
☐ 情緒安定性	emotional stability
☐ 象徴	symbol
☐ 象徴主義	symbolism
☐ 情緒的意味	affective meaning
☐ 照度	illuminance
☐ 衝動	impulse
☐ **情動**	**emotion; affect**
☐ 情動価	emotional valence
☐ 情動条件づけ	emotional conditioning
☐ 情動焦点型コーピング	emotion-focused coping
☐ 情動神経科学	affective neuroscience
☐ 常同性	stereotype

☐ 情動制御	emotion regulation
☐ 情動摂食	emotional eating
☐ 情動知能	emotional intelligence
☐ 情動反応	emotional response
☐ 承認	approval
☐ 情熱	passion
☐ 情熱的な愛	passionate love
☐ 小脳	cerebellum
☐ 情報	information
☐ **情報処理**	**information processing**
☐ 情報処理モデル	information-processing model
☐ 情報勢力	informational power
☐ 情報理論	information theory
☐ 譲歩の要請法	door-in-the-face-technique
☐ 剰余変数	extraneous variable
☐ 省略訓練	omission training
☐ 症例コントロール研究	case control study
☐ 初期経験	early experience
☐ 処遇	treatment
☐ 食餌性条件づけ	appetitive conditioning
☐ 触発子	releaser
☐ 触発刺激	releasing stimulus
☐ 食物嗜好	food preference
☐ 食物歴	food history
☐ 初語	first word
☐ 叙述的文献研究	narrative review
☐ 女性性	femininity
☐ 所属機関	affiliation
☐ 所属性	belongingness
☐ 処置	treatment
☐ 初潮	menarche
☐ 触覚	tactile sensation
☐ 初頭効果	primacy effect

☐ 徐波睡眠	slow wave sleep, SWS
☐ 処理水準	levels of processing
☐ 処理陰性電位	processing negativity, PN
☐ 処理様式説	processing mode theory
☐ 処理容量	processing capacity
☐ **序論**	**introduction**
☐ 自律訓練法	autogenic training
☐ **自律神経系**	**autonomic nervous system, ANS**
☐ 自律性	autonomy
☐ 自律反応	autonomic response
☐ 視力	visual acuity
☐ 事例	instance
☐ **事例研究**	**case study**
☐ 事例史	case history
☐ ジレンマ	dilemma
☐ 心因反応	psychogenetic reaction
☐ **人格**	**personality**
☐ 人格障害	personality disorder
☐ 人格心理学	personality psychology
☐ 人格目録	personality inventory
☐ 進化心理学	evolutionary psychology
☐ **進化論**	**theory of evolution**
☐ 心気症	hypochondriasis
☐ 新奇性恐怖	neophobia
☐ 親近性	familiarity
☐ 新近性効果	recency effect
☐ **神経**	**nerve**
☐ 神経核	nucleus
☐ 神経過敏性	neural sensitization
☐ **神経系**	**nervous system**
☐ **神経細胞**	**neuron**
☐ 神経支配	innervation
☐ 神経症	neurosis（複数：neuroses）

☐ 神経修飾物質	neuromodulator
☐ 神経症の傾向	neuroticism
☐ 神経症的不安	neurotic anxiety
☐ 神経心理学	neuropsychology
☐ 神経性過食症	bulimia nervosa
☐ 神経性無食欲症	anorexia nervosa
☐ 神経生理学	neurophysiology
☐ 神経節	ganglia（単数：ganglion）
☐ 神経伝達物質	neurotransmitter
☐ 神経伝導	nerve conduction
☐ 神経網	neural network
☐ 神経モデル	neuronal model
☐ **信号**	**signal**
☐ 信号検出理論	signal detection theory, SDT
☐ 信号刺激	signal stimulus
☐ 人工知能	artificial intelligence
☐ 信号追跡	sign tracking
☐ 新行動主義	neobehaviorism
☐ 進行マヒ	general paresis
☐ 心誌	psychograph
☐ 真実性	genuineness; realness
☐ 心身医学	psychosomatic medicine
☐ 心身症	psychosomatic disease; psychosomatic disorder
☐ 心身同型説	psychophysical isomorphism
☐ 心身二元論	dualism
☐ 心身の	psychosomatic
☐ 新生児	neonate
☐ 新精神分析学派	neo-analytic theorist
☐ 人生満足度尺度	Life Satisfaction Index, LSI
☐ 振せん	tremor
☐ **心像**	**image**; imagery; mental image
☐ 深層構造	deep structure

用語（和→英） しょ〜しん

☐ 身体像, 身体的自己	body image
☐ 身体的な健康	physical health
☐ 身体的魅力	physical attractiveness
☐ 診断	diagnosis
☐ 診断的面接	interview for diagnosis
☐ 心的イメージ	mental image
☐ **心的外傷**	**trauma**
☐ **心的外傷後ストレス障害**	**posttraumatic stress disorder, PTSD**
☐ 心的回転	mental rotation
☐ 心的活動	mental activity
☐ 心的過程	mental process
☐ 心的表象	mental representation
☐ 心的負荷	mental workload
☐ 心的分泌	psychic secretion
☐ 心的飽和	psychological satiation
☐ 心電図	electrocardiogram, ECG
☐ 振動体	oscillator
☐ 真にランダムな統制条件	truly random control, TRC
☐ 信念	belief
☐ 心拍	heart beat
☐ 心拍間隔	interbeat interval, IBI
☐ **心拍数, 心拍率**	**heart rate, HR**
☐ 心拍(率)変動	heart rate variability, HRV
☐ 新皮質	neocortex
☐ 振幅	amplitude
☐ 新フロイト派	neo-Freudian
☐ シンボリズム	symbolism
☐ シンボル	symbol
☐ 親密性	intimacy
☐ 信頼区間	confidence interval
☐ **信頼性**	**reliability**
☐ **心理学**	**psychology**

☐ 心理学者	psychologist
☐ 心理学的決定論	psychological determinism
☐ 心理言語学	psycholinguistics
☐ 心理検査	psychological test
☐ 心理神経免疫学	psychoneuroimmunology
☐ 心理生理学	psychophysiology
☐ 心理生理的障害	psychophysiological disorder
☐ 心理的ストレス反応尺度	Psychological Stress Response Scale, PSRS
☐ 心理的等価性	psychological equivalence
☐ 心理テスト	psychological test
☐ 心理物理学	psychophysics
☐ 心理物理関数	psychophysical function
☐ 心理物理同型説	psychophysical isomorphism
☐ 心理変数	psychological variable
☐ 心理力動	psychodynamics
☐ **心理療法**	**psychotherapy**
☐ 人類学	anthropology
☐ 親和葛藤	affiliative conflict
☐ 親和動機	affiliation motive
☐ 図	figure
☐ 随意(の)	voluntary
☐ 随意活動	voluntary activity; voluntary movement
☐ 随意行動	voluntary behavior
☐ 随意制御	voluntary control
☐ 随意性瞬目	voluntary blink
☐ 随意反応	voluntary response
☐ 遂行	performance
☐ 遂行の知識	knowledge of performance, KP
☐ 水準	level
☐ **推測統計(学)**	**inferential statistics**
☐ 錐体	cone

☐ 吸いつき反射	sucking reflex
☐ 垂直眼球運動	vertical eye movement
☐ スイッチング	switching
☐ 随伴陰性電位	contingent negative variation, CNV
☐ **随伴性**	**contingency**
☐ 随伴性空間	contingency space
☐ 随伴性契約	contingency contracting
☐ 随伴性判断	contingency judgement
☐ 水平眼球運動	horizontal eye movement
☐ **睡眠**	**sleep**
☐ 睡眠経過図	sleep histogram
☐ 睡眠周期	sleep cycle
☐ 睡眠障害	sleep disorder
☐ 睡眠段階	sleep stage
☐ 睡眠内周期	intra sleep cycle
☐ 睡眠変数	sleep variable
☐ 睡眠紡錘波	sleep spindle
☐ 推理	inference; reasoning
☐ **推論**	**inference**
☐ 数量化理論	quantification theory
☐ 数量的データ	quantitative data
☐ スキナー箱，スキナー・ボックス	Skinner box
☐ **スキーマ**	**schema**
☐ スキーマティック処理	schematic processing
☐ スキャロップ現象	scallop
☐ スキル	skill
☐ スクリプト	script
☐ スケール	scale
☐ 図式	schema
☐ スタンバーグ記憶走査課題	Sternberg memory-scanning task
☐ スタンフォード眠気尺度	Stanford Sleepiness Scale, SSS

☐ スタンフォード・ビネー知能検査	Stanford-Binet Intelligence Scale
☐ スティーブンスの法則	Stevens' law
☐ ステレオタイプ	stereotype
☐ 図と地	figure-ground
☐ ストループ干渉	Stroop interference
☐ **ストループ効果**	**Stroop effect**
☐ ストレージ	storage
☐ **ストレス**	**stress**
☐ ストレス脆弱性モデル	vulnerability-stress model
☐ **ストレス対処**, ストレス・コーピング	**stress coping**
☐ ストレス反応	stress response
☐ ストレス・マネジメント	stress management
☐ **ストレッサー**	**stressor**
☐ ストレンジ・シチュエーション法	strange situation procedure
☐ ストロボスコープ運動	stroboscopic motion
☐ スネレン視力	Snellen acuity
☐ スーパーヴァイザー	supervisor
☐ スーパーヴィジョン	supervision
☐ スーパーエゴ	superego
☐ スピーチセラピスト	speech therapist, ST
☐ 刷り込み	imprinting
☐ 性	gender; sex
☐ 斉一性	uniformity
☐ 斉一性への圧力	pressure to uniformity
☐ 成員	member
☐ **性格**	**character**
☐ 生活上の出来事	life event
☐ **生活体**	**organism**
☐ 生活年齢	chronological age, CA
☐ 生活の質	quality of life, QOL
☐ 性器期	genital stage

☐ 正規性	normality
☐ **正規分布**	**normal distribution**
☐ **制御**	**control**
☐ 制御可能性	controllability
☐ 生産	production
☐ 生産欠如	production deficiency
☐ 生産性	productivity
☐ 生産的思考	productive thinking
☐ **制止**	**inhibition**
☐ 制止子	inhibitor
☐ 制止条件づけ	inhibitory conditioning
☐ 誠実性	conscientiousness
☐ 静止膜電位	resting membrane potential
☐ **成熟**	**maturation; maturity**
☐ 正常	normality
☐ **精神医学**	**psychiatry**
☐ 精神衛生	mental health
☐ 精神科医	psychiatrist
☐ 精神活性薬	psychoactive drug
☐ 精神活動	mental activity
☐ 精神過程	mental process
☐ 精神間	interpsychic
☐ **成人期**	**adulthood**
☐ 精神健康調査票	General Health Questionnaire, GHQ
☐ 精神時間測定法	mental chronometry
☐ 精神疾患	mental disorder
☐ 精神疾患の診断・統計マニュアル,DSM	Diagnostic and Statistical Manual of Mental Disorders, DSM
☐ 精神障害	mental disorder
☐ **精神生理学**	**psychophysiology**
☐ 精神遅滞	mental retardation
☐ 精神遅滞者	mentally retarded

精神的健康	mental health
精神的分泌	psychic secretion
精神内の	intrapsychic
精神年齢	mental age, MA
精神病	psychosis(複数:psychoses)
精神病質	psychopathy
精神病的傾向	psychoticism
精神病理学	psychopathology
精神負荷	mental workload
精神物理学	**psychophysics**
精神分析(学)	**psychoanalysis**
精神分析理論	psychoanalytic theory
精神薬理学	psychopharmacology
精神力動	**psychodynamics**
精神力動の療法	psychodynamic therapy
性心理的段階	psychosexual stages
生成効果	generation effect
生成文法	generative grammar
成績	performance
生前の意思表示書	living will
生存	survival
生体外測定法	in vitro measurement
生態学的自己	ecological self
生態学的妥当性	ecological validity
生態光学	ecological optics
生体恒常性	homeostasis
生体恒常的睡眠動因	homeostatic sleep drive
生態的地位	ecological niche
生体内測定法	in vivo measurement
精緻化	elaboration
精緻化見込みモデル	elaboration likelihood model
精緻化リハーサル	elaborative rehearsal
性的刻印づけ	sexual imprinting

☐ 性的志向	sexual orientation
☐ 性的衝動	sexual urge
☐ 性的刷り込み	sexual imprinting
☐ 性同一性障害	gender identity disorder
☐ 正当勢力	legitimate power
☐ 性淘汰	sexual selection
☐ 生得主義,生得説	nativism
☐ 生得的傾向	predisposition
☐ 生得的行動	innate behavior
☐ 生得的触発機構	innate releasing mechanism, IRM
☐ 青年期	**adolescence**
☐ 青年期発達加速	adolescent growth spurt
☐ 性の型づけ	sex typing
☐ 正の強化	positive reinforcement
☐ 正の相関関係	positive correlation
☐ 正の転移	positive transfer
☐ 正の罰	positive punishment
☐ 正のフィードバック	positive feedback
☐ 生の本能	life instinct
☐ 正否定《信号検出理論の》	correct rejection
☐ 正比例	direct proportion
☐ 生物医学モデル	biomedical model
☐ 生物心理学	biological psychology
☐ 生物心理社会モデル	biopsychosocial model
☐ 生物時計	biological clock
☐ 生物〔生体〕リズム	biological rhythm
☐ 性役割	sex role
☐ 生理学	**physiology**
☐ 生理心理学	**physiological psychology**
☐ 生理的早産	physiological premature delivery
☐ 生理的平衡	homeostasis
☐ 勢力構造	power structure
☐ 脊髄	spinal cord

☐	脊髄反射	spinal reflex
☐	責任の拡散，責任の分散	diffusion of responsibility
☐	舌下腺	sublingual gland
☐	積極性相互作用	proactive interaction
☐	積極的傾聴	active listening
☐	**接近**	**approach**
☐	接近-回避葛藤	approach-avoidance conflict
☐	接近可能性	accessibility
☐	接近-接近葛藤	approach-approach conflict
☐	接近の法則	law of contiguity
☐	セックス	sex
☐	接種理論	inoculation theory
☐	摂食障害	eating disorder
☐	摂食中枢	feeding center
☐	絶対閾	absolute threshold
☐	舌端現象	tip of the tongue phenomenon
☐	折衷的アプローチ	eclectic approach
☐	設定値	set point
☐	節点	node
☐	説得	persuasion
☐	z 得点	z score
☐	折半法信頼性	split-half reliability
☐	説明責任	accountability
☐	説明を受けた上での承諾	informed consent
☐	節約の法則	law of parsimony
☐	セマンティック・ディファレンシャル法	semantic differential method
☐	セルフケア	self-care
☐	セルフ・ハンディキャッピング	self-handicapping
☐	セルフ・マネジメント	self-management
☐	セルフ・モニタリング	self-monitoring
☐	セロトニン	serotonin
☐	セロトニン再取り込み阻害薬	serotonin reuptake inhibitors

☐ ゼロ和ゲーム	zero-sum game
☐ 腺	gland
☐ 前意識	preconsciousness
☐ 前期高齢者	young-old
☐ 線型	linear
☐ 前件	antecedent
☐ 宣言型記憶，宣言的記憶	declarative memory
☐ 宣言型知識，宣言的知識	declarative knowledge
☐ 閃光記憶	flashbulb memory
☐ 先行刺激	antecedent; prime
☐ 選好性	preference
☐ 前向性健忘	anterograde amnesia
☐ 選好注視法	preference-looking technique
☐ 潜在意識	subconsciousness
☐ 潜在学習	implicit leaning; latent learning
☐ 潜在記憶	implicit memory
☐ 潜在行動	**covert behavior**
☐ 潜在内容	latent content
☐ 潜時	latency
☐ 漸次的接近	successive approximation
☐ 漸次的接近法	method of successive approximation
☐ 染色体	chromosome
☐ 漸進的筋弛緩法	progressive muscle relaxation
☐ 前操作段階〔期〕	preoperational stage〔period〕
☐ 全体的行動	molar behavior
☐ 全体報告条件	whole-report condition
☐ 全体論	holism〔wholism〕
☐ 全体論的思考	holistic thought
☐ 選択性緘黙	selective mutism
☐ 選択的強化	selective reinforcement
☐ 選択的順応	selective adaptation
☐ 選択的注意	**selective attention**

☐ 選択反応時間	choice reaction time, CRT
☐ 前注意過程	preattentive process
☐ 前頭正中部θ波	frontal midline theta, Fm θ
☐ 前頭前野	prefrontal lobe
☐ 前頭葉	frontal lobe
☐ 先入観，先入見	preoccupation
☐ 前認知的感情	precognitive emotion
☐ 全般不安症，全般性不安障害	generalized anxiety disorder
☐ 潜伏期	latency period
☐ せん妄	delirium
☐ 素因	predisposition
☐ 躁うつ精神病	manic-depressive psychosis
☐ 躁うつ病	manic-depressive illness
☐ **相関，相関関係**	**correlation**
☐ **相関係数**	**correlation coefficient**
☐ 相関研究	correlational study
☐ 相関図	scatter diagram
☐ 相関法	correlational method
☐ 双極性障害	bipolar disorder
☐ 相互依存性	interdependency
☐ **相互作用**	**interaction**
☐ 相互作用過程分析	interactional process analysis, IPA
☐ 相互心理的	interpsychic
☐ **操作**	**manipulation**; operation
☐ 走査	scan
☐ 操作子	operator
☐ 操作主義	operationism
☐ 操作的定義	operational definition
☐ 早産児	preterm infant
☐ 躁状態	manic state
☐ 走性	taxis
☐ **総説**	**review**
☐ 創造性	creativity

☐ 創造的思考	creative thinking
☐ 相対リスク	relative risk
☐ 相反過程説	opponent-process theory
☐ 躁病	mania
☐ 層別標本	stratified sample
☐ 相貌失認	prosopagnosia
☐ 促進	facilitation
☐ 属性(への)帰属	dispositional attribution
☐ **測定**	**measurement**
☐ **測度**	**measure**
☐ 側頭葉	temporal lobe
☐ 速度と正確さのトレードオフ	speed-accuracy trade-off
☐ 側面	facet
☐ 側抑制	lateral inhibition
☐ 阻止	blocking
☐ ソシオグラム	sociogram
☐ ソシオマトリクス	sociomatrix
☐ ソシオメトリー	sociometry
☐ ソシオメトリック構造	sociometric structure
☐ ソシオメトリック・テスト	sociometric test
☐ 組織	organization
☐ 組織心理学	organizational psychology
☐ ソーシャルサポート	social support
☐ ソーシャルスキル	social skill
☐ ソーシャルスキルトレーニング	social skills training, SST
☐ 素性	feature
☐ 率先的相互作用	proactive interaction
☐ 素点, 粗点	raw score
☐ 素朴実在論	naive realism
☐ 素朴心理学	naive psychology
☐ ソロモン計画	Solomon's design
☐ ソーンダイク型条件づけ	Thorndikean conditioning

た 行

第一印象	first impression
第一次予防	primary prevention
第1種の誤り〔過誤〕	error of type I; type I error
大〔単極性〕うつ病	major 〔unipolar〕 depression
対応推測理論	correspondent inference theory
対応性	correspondence
体温	body temperature
大学進学適性検査	Scholastic Assessment Test
退行	regression
第三次予防	tertiary prevention
胎児期	fetal period
対処	**coping**
対象化理論	objectification theory
対象関係論	object relations theory
対照群	**control group**
対照条件	contrast condition
代償的反応	substitute response
対象の永続性	object permanence
対人関係療法	interpersonal therapy
対人関係論	interpersonal theory
対人スキル	interpersonal skill
対人的回避	interpersonal repulsion
対人認知	interpersonal cognition
対人魅力	interpersonal attraction
耐性	**tolerance**
大数の法則	law of large numbers
体制化	organization
体性感覚	somatosensory
体性神経系	somatic nervous system
大多数者集団	majority
態度	**attitude**
対等化法	pair matching

☐ 態度のバランス理論	balance theory of attitude
☐ 第2種の誤り〔過誤〕	error of type II; type II error
☐ 第二次予防	secondary prevention
☐ 大脳	cerebrum
☐ 大脳化	encephalization
☐ 大脳半球	cerebral hemisphere
☐ **大脳皮質**	**cerebral cortex**
☐ 大脳辺縁系	limbic system
☐ 大脳誘発電位	cerebral evoked potential, cerebral EP
☐ 対比	contrast
☐ 退避	withdrawal
☐ 対比視力	contrast acuity
☐ 代表性ヒューリスティック	representativeness heuristic
☐ タイプA行動	Type A behavior
☐ 大麻	cannabis
☐ タイムアウト	time out
☐ 対面集団	face-to-face group
☐ 代理学習	vicarious learning
☐ 代理強化	vicarious reinforcement
☐ 代理条件づけ	vicarious conditioning
☐ 代理症状	symptom substitute
☐ 対立仮説	alternative hypothesis
☐ ダウン症候群	Down syndrome
☐ 唾液	saliva
☐ 唾液分泌	salivation
☐ 多感覚様相的注意	multimodal attention
☐ ターゲット,ターゲット項目	target
☐ 多元的無知,多数の無知	pluralistic ignorance
☐ 多元ベースライン計画法	multiple-baseline design
☐ 多次元尺度構成法	multi-dimensional scale, MDS
☐ 多肢選択法	multiple choice method
☐ 多重人格	multiple personality

☐ 多重操作	multiple operation
☐ 多重測定	multiple measurement
☐ 多重知能	multiple intelligence, MI
☐ 多重貯蔵モデル	multistore model
☐ 多重比較	multiple comparison
☐ 多種反応測定記録装置	polygraph
☐ 脱感作	desensitization
☐ 脱施設化	deinstitutionalization
☐ 脱馴化, 脱慣れ	dishabituation
☐ 達成動機	achievement motive
☐ 脱物質主義	postmaterialist
☐ 脱抑制	disinhibition
☐ 縦軸	vertical axis
☐ 妥当化	validation
☐ 多動性	hyperactivity
☐ **妥当性**	**validity**
☐ 妥当性検証	validation
☐ タナトス《死の本能》	Thanatos
☐ タフ・マインド傾向	tough-mindedness
☐ タブラ・ラサ	tabula rasa
☐ ダブルバーレル質問	double barreled question
☐ 多変量解析	multivariate analysis
☐ 多変量実験	multivariate experiment
☐ 単一回答式質問	closed-ended question
☐ 単一恐怖	simple phobia
☐ 単一事例実験	single-case experiment
☐ 単一被験者〔被験体〕研究	single-subject experiment
☐ 段階	phase
☐ 段階の教示	programmed instruction
☐ 段階的変化モデル	stage of change model
☐ 段階的要請法	foot-in-the-door technique
☐ **短期記憶**	**short-term memory, STM**
☐ 短期心理療法	brief psychotherapy

☐ 短期貯蔵庫	short-term store, STS
☐ 短期療法	brief therapy
☐ 男根期	phallic stage
☐ 探索的因子分析	exploratory factor analysis, EFA
☐ 探索的データ解析	exploratory data analysis, EDA
☐ 探索反射	searching reflex
☐ 単純細胞	simple cell
☐ 単純接触効果	mere exposure effect
☐ 単純反応時間	simple reaction time, SRT
☐ 単純盲検法	single-blind test〔design, procedure, technique〕
☐ 男性性	masculinity
☐ 談話療法	talking cure
☐ 地位	status
☐ 地域社会	community
☐ 知恵	wisdom
☐ **知覚**	**perception**
☐ 知覚運動学習	perceptual-motor learning
☐ 知覚学習	perceptual learning
☐ 知覚〔感覚〕神経	sensory nerve
☐ 知覚的構え	perceptual set
☐ 知覚的干渉	perceptual interference
☐ 知覚的体制化	perceptual organization
☐ 知覚的防衛	perceptual defence
☐ 知覚の恒常性	perceptual constancy
☐ 置換説	substitution theory
☐ 知識	knowledge
☐ 知性化	intellectualization
☐ 遅滞法	retardation method
☐ チック	tic
☐ **知能**	**intelligence**
☐ 知能検査	intelligence test
☐ 知能指数	intelligence quotient, IQ

☐ 知能の三部理論	triarchic theory of intelligence
☐ チームワーク	teamwork
☐ チャンキング	chunking
☐ チャンク	chunk
☐ **注意**	**attention**
☐ 注意欠如・多動症〔障害〕	attention deficit/hyperactivity disorder, ADHD
☐ 注意痕跡説	attentional trace
☐ 注意説	attention theory
☐ 注意の逸脱	distraction
☐ **中央値**	**median**
☐ 中間施設	halfway house
☐ 注視点	fixation point
☐ 中耳	middle ear
☐ 抽出誤差	sampling error
☐ 抽象(的)	abstract
☐ 抽象化	abstraction
☐ 中心窩	fovea
☐ 中心化傾向	central tendency
☐ 中心経路	central route
☐ 中心転換	recentering
☐ **中枢神経系**	**central nervous system, CNS**
☐ 中枢的動機状態	central motive state
☐ **中性刺激**	**neutral stimulus, NS**
☐ 中脳	mesencephalon; midbrain
☐ **聴覚**	**audition**
☐ 聴覚系	auditory system
☐ 聴覚的手がかり	auditory cue
☐ 超感覚的知覚, 超能力	extrasensory perception, ESP
☐ **長期記憶**	**long-term memory, LTM**
☐ 長期増強	long-term potentiation
☐ 長期貯蔵庫	long-term store, LTS
☐ 長期抑圧	long-term depression

☐ 徴候	symptom
☐ **調査**	**survey**
☐ 調査票	questionnaire
☐ 調査法	survey method
☐ 超自我	superego
☐ 長日周期	infradian rhythm
☐ 超常現象	psi
☐ 超心理学	parapsychology
☐ (水晶体の)調整作用	accommodation
☐ 超正常刺激	supernormal stimulus
☐ 調整ヒューリスティック	adjustment heuristic
☐ 調整変数	moderator variable
☐ 調整法	method of adjustment
☐ 調節	accommodation
☐ 挑戦	challenge
☐ 頂点位相	acrophase
☐ 丁度可知差異	just noticeable difference, jnd
☐ 超能力	psychic power
☐ 超能力者	psychic
☐ 跳躍伝動	saltatory conduction
☐ 調和性	agreeableness
☐ 直後記憶	immediate memory
☐ 直後強化	immediate reinforcement
☐ 直接観察	direct observation
☐ 直接記憶範囲	immediate memory span
☐ 直線形	linear
☐ 直線走路	straight alley
☐ 直喩	simile
☐ 直列型処理	serial processing
☐ 直列探索	serial search
☐ 著作権	copyright; credit
☐ 著者	author
☐ **貯蔵**	**storage**

☐ 貯蔵段階	storage stage	
☐ 直観像	eidetic image	
☐ 直観	intuition	
☐ 直交	orthogonal	
☐ **治療**	**treatment**	
☐ 鎮痛薬	opiates	
☐ **追試**	**replication**	
☐ 追従	compliance	
☐ 追従運動, 追従眼球運動	smooth pursuit	
☐ 追従者	follower	
☐ 追唱	shadowing	
☐ 追跡	tracking	
☐ 追跡研究	follow-up study	
☐ 対連合法	paired associates method	
☐ 痛覚	pain	
☐ 通常脳波	ongoing EEG; routine EEG	
☐ 強さ	intensity	
☐ 定位	orientation	
☐ **定位反射**	**orienting reflex, OR**	
☐ 定位反応	orienting response	
☐ 定義的特性	defining feature	
☐ **t検定**	**t-test**	
☐ 抵抗	resistance	
☐ 抵抗期	stage of resistance	
☐ 定常状態	steady state	
☐ ディストラクター	distractor	
☐ ディセプション	deception	
☐ T得点	T score	
☐ 低反応率分化強化スケジュール	differential reinforcement of low rate, DRL	
☐ ディープライム《信号検出理論の》	d'	
☐ 提喩	synecdoche	

☐ 手がかり	cue
☐ 敵意	hostility
☐ 敵意ある攻撃性	hostile aggression
☐ **適応**	**adaptation**
☐ 適応行動	adaptive behavior
☐ 適合性	congruity
☐ 適者生存	survival of the fittest
☐ 適性	aptitude
☐ 敵対者	antagonist
☐ 的中《信号検出理論の》	hit
☐ デコーディング	decoding
☐ デシベル尺度	decibel scale
☐ テスト	test
☐ テスト・バッテリー	test battery
☐ テスト不安	test anxiety
☐ データ駆動型処理	data-driven processing
☐ 哲学	philosophy
☐ **手続き**	**procedure**; operation
☐ 手続き型知識	procedural knowledge
☐ **手続き的記憶**	**procedural memory**
☐ 徹底的行動主義	radical behaviorism
☐ 手のばし行動	reaching
☐ デブリーフィング	debriefing
☐ デマ	demagogy
☐ デルタ波	δ wave
☐ テレプレゼンス	telepresence
☐ 転移	transference
☐ てんかん	epilepsy
☐ 転換性障害	conversion disorder
☐ 電気けいれん療法	electroconvulsive therapy, ECT
☐ 電気ショック	electric shock
☐ 電極	electrode
☐ 典型性	typicality

☐ 電撃	electric shock
☐ 天才	gifted
☐ 天井効果	ceiling effect
☐ 電文体発話	telegraphic speech
☐ 展望	perspective; review
☐ 展望的記憶	prospective memory
☐ ドア・イン・ザ・フェイス法	door-in-the-face-technique
☐ 同一化	identification
☐ **動因**	**drive**
☐ 動因低減	drive reduction
☐ 動因低減説	drive reduction theory
☐ 動因理論	drive theory
☐ **投影検査，投映検査**	**projective test**
☐ 投影法，投映法	projective technique
☐ 同化	assimilation
☐ 統覚	apperception
☐ 等価性	equipotentiality
☐ 動機	motive
☐ **動機づけ**	**motivation**
☐ 動機の葛藤	conflict of motives
☐ 道具的学習	instrumental learning
☐ 道具的攻撃	instrumental aggression
☐ **道具的条件づけ**	**instrumental conditioning**
☐ **統計学**	**statistics**
☐ 統計的検定	statistical test
☐ 統計的有意性	statistical significance
☐ 統計モデル	statistical model
☐ 統語	syntax
☐ 瞳孔	pupil
☐ 登校拒否	school refusal
☐ 瞳孔計	pupillometry
☐ 統合失調症	schizophrenia
☐ 瞳孔反射	pupillary reflex

☐ 動作性検査	performance test
☐ **洞察**	**insight**
☐ 洞察療法	insight therapy
☐ 同時条件づけ	simultaneous conditioning
☐ 同質性	homogeneity
☐ 投射	projection
☐ 等色実験	color matching experiment
☐ **統制**	**control**
☐ 統制可能性	controllability
☐ **統制群**	**control group**
☐ 統制刺激	controlled stimulation
☐ 統制条件	control condition
☐ 統制的処理〔過程〕	control process
☐ 統制の位置，統制の所在	locus of control, LOC
☐ 逃走	fleeing
☐ 闘争	fighting
☐ 闘争・逃走反応	fight-or-flight response
☐ 同調	conformity
☐ 同調傾向	synchrony
☐ 頭頂葉	parietal lobe
☐ 動的知覚	dynamic perception
☐ 道徳的判断	moral judgment
☐ 導入(部)	introduction
☐ **逃避**	**escape**
☐ 逃避学習	escape learning
☐ 逃避行動	escape behavior
☐ 頭部外傷	head injury
☐ 動物行動学	ethology
☐ 動物行動学者	ethologist
☐ 読字障害	dyslexia
☐ 特殊(知能)因子	specific (intelligence) factor
☐ 特殊飢餓	specific hunger
☐ **特性**	**trait**

□ 特性比較モデル	feature comparison model
□ 独創性	originality
□ 特徴	feature
□ 特徴的特性	characteristic feature
□ 特徴統合理論	feature integration theory
□ 特定文脈効果	specific context effect
□ 匿名性	anonymity
□ **独立変数**	**independent variable**
□ トークン・エコノミー	token economy
□ 度数	frequency
□ **度数分布**	**frequency distribution**
□ **トップダウン処理**	**top-down processing**
□ トップダウン・フィードバック結合	top-down feedback connections
□ ドーパミン	dopamine
□ トポグラフ	topograph
□ **トラウマ**	**trauma**
□ トラッキング	tracking
□ 取り引き	bargaining
□ ドリフト	drift

な 行

□ 内因性精神病	endogenous psychosis
□ 内因性電位	endogenous potentials
□ **内観**	**introspection**
□ 内言	inner speech
□ 内言化段階	ingrowth stage
□ 内向型	introvert
□ **内向性**	**introversion**
□ 内在化	internalization
□ 内集団	in-group
□ **内省**	**introspection**

☐ 内臓知覚	visceral perception
☐ 内臓反応	visceral response
☐ 内側膝状体	medial geniculate body
☐ 内的一貫性	internal consistency
☐ 内的葛藤	internal conflict
☐ 内的整合性	internal consistency
☐ 内的脱同調	internal desynchronization
☐ 内的妥当性	internal validity
☐ 内的統制	internal control
☐ 内発的動機づけ	intrinsic motivation
☐ 内罰的反応	intropunitive responce
☐ 内分泌	endocrine
☐ 内包的意味	connotative meaning
☐ 仲間集団	peer group
☐ 生のデータ	raw data
☐ ナラティブ・アプローチ	narrative approach
☐ ナルコレプシー	narcolepsy
☐ ナルシシズム	narcissism
☐ ナルトレキソン	naltrexone
☐ 慣れの効果	habituation effect
☐ 喃語	babbling
☐ 二元論	dualism
☐ 二項分布	binominal distribution
☐ 二次強化	secondary reinforcement
☐ 二次集団	secondary group
☐ 二次条件づけ	second-order conditioning
☐ 二次性強化子	secondary reinforcer
☐ 二次的動因	secondary drive
☐ 二次的評価	secondary appraisal
☐ 二重課題	dual task
☐ 二重作業	dual task
☐ 二重符号化仮説	dual coding hypothesis

☐ 二重盲検法	**double-blind test〔design; procedure; technique〕**
☐ 二色型色覚	dichromatism
☐ 日常いらだち事	daily hassles
☐ 日常記憶	everyday memory
☐ 日常生活動作	activity of daily living, ADL
☐ 乳児期	infancy
☐ 入眠時レム	sleep onset REM episode
☐ 乳(幼)児	infant
☐ ニューラル・ネットワーク	neural network
☐ ニューロン	neuron
☐ 二要因理論	two-factor theory
☐ 二卵性双生児	dizygotic twins
☐ 人間工学	ergonomics; human factors
☐ 人間主義者	humanist
☐ 人間性心理学	humanistic psychology
☐ 人間性療法	humanistic therapy
☐ 人間中心療法	person centered therapy
☐ **認知**	**cognition**
☐ 認知閾	recognition threshold
☐ 認知科学	cognitive science
☐ 認知学習	cognitive learning
☐ 認知過程	cognitive process
☐ **認知行動療法**	**cognitive behavior therapy, CBT**
☐ 認知症	dementia
☐ 認知神経科学	cognitive neuroscience
☐ **認知心理学**	**cognitive psychology**
☐ 認知地図	cognitive map
☐ 認知的アプローチ	cognitive approach
☐ 認知的経済性	cognitive economy
☐ 認知的再構成	cognitive restructuring
☐ 認知的斉合性	cognitive consistency
☐ 認知的評価	cognitive appraisal

☐ **認知的不協和理論**	**cognitive dissonance theory**
☐ 認知療法	cognitive therapy, CT
☐ 音色	timbre
☐ 熱愛	passionate love
☐ 熱情	passion
☐ ネットワーク・モデル	network model
☐ 眠気	drowsiness
☐ ノイズ	noise
☐ **脳**	**brain**
☐ 脳画像法	brain imaging
☐ 脳幹	brain stem
☐ 脳幹電位	brainstem potential
☐ 脳幹反応	brain stem response, BSR
☐ 脳幹網様体	brainstem reticular formation
☐ 脳血管障害	cerebral vascular accident
☐ 脳梗塞	cerebral infarction
☐ 脳磁図	magnetoencephalogram, MEG
☐ 脳出血	cerebral hemorrhage
☐ 脳脊髄神経(系)	cranial and spinal nerves
☐ 脳電気活動	electrical brain activity
☐ 脳電図	electroencephalogram, EEG
☐ 能動的注意	active attention
☐ **脳波**	**electroencephalogram, EEG;** brain wave
☐ 脳梁	fornix
☐ 能力	competence
☐ ノード	node
☐ のどまで出かかる現象	tip of the tongue phenomenon
☐ ノーマライゼーション	normalization
☐ ノルアドレナリン	noradrenaline, NA
☐ ノルエピネフリン	norepinephrine, NE
☐ ノンパラメトリック法	nonparametric method
☐ ノンレム睡眠	non-REM sleep, NREM sleep

は 行

把握反射	grasping reflex
バイアス	**bias**
バイオフィードバック	**biofeedback, BF**
バイオロジカルモーション	biological motion
媒介	mediation
媒介体	mediator
媒介変数	intervening variable
媒介理論	mediation theory
背景脳波	background EEG
場依存性	field dependence
ハイブリッド	hybrid
パイロット・スタディ	pilot study
パイロット・テスト	pilot test
バウムテスト	Baumtest; tree drawing test
パーキンソン病	Parkinson's disease
白紙状態	tabula rasa
白質	white matter
白色ノイズ	white noise
剥奪	deprivation
白昼夢	daydream
拍動間隔	interbeat interval, IBI
暴露療法	exposure therapy
箱庭療法	sandplay technique
場所法	method of loci
橋渡しの推論	bridging inference
外れ値	outlier
派生的動機	derived motive
パーセプトロン	perceptron
パーセンタイル順位	percentile rank
パーセンタイル点	percentile score
パーソナリティ	**personality**
パーソナリティ障害	personality disorder

☐ パーソナリティ心理学	personality psychology
☐ パーソナル・コンストラクト	personal construct
☐ パーソナル・スペース	personal space
☐ パターン認識	pattern recognition
☐ 恥	shame
☐ **罰**	**punishment**
☐ 発汗	perspiration
☐ バック・プロパゲーション	back propagation
☐ 発散的思考	divergent thinking
☐ 発生率	incidence
☐ **発達**	**development**
☐ 発達加速現象	developmet(al) acceleration
☐ 発達症〔障害〕	developmental disorder
☐ **発達心理学**	**developmental psychology**
☐ 発達段階	stages of development
☐ 発達の最近接領域	zone of proximal development
☐ 発揚	excitement
☐ 発話行為	speech act
☐ ハーディネス	hardiness
☐ ハーディネス・パーソナリティ特性	hardy personality
☐ パニック	panic
☐ パニック症〔障害〕	panic disorder
☐ パニック発作	panic attack
☐ 跳ね返り	rebound
☐ 場の理論	field theory
☐ ハハァ経験	aha experience
☐ バビンスキー反射	Babinski reflex
☐ パフォーマンス	performance
☐ パブロフ型条件づけ	Pavlovian conditioning
☐ 場面緘黙症	selective mutism
☐ パラコントラスト	paracontrast
☐ パラダイム	paradigm

☐ パラノイア	paranoia
☐ パラフレニア	paraphrenia
☐ パラメータ	parameter
☐ パラメトリック法	parametric method
☐ バランス	balance
☐ ハロー効果	halo-effect
☐ 範囲	range
☐ 反映	reflection
☐ **般化**	**generalization**
☐ 般化勾配	generalization gradient
☐ 半球	hemisphere
☐ 反響言語	echolalia
☐ 半構造化面接	semi-structured interview
☐ 犯罪心理学	criminal psychology
☐ **反射**	**reflex**; reflection
☐ 反社会性パーソナリティ	antisocial personality
☐ 反社会的行動	antisocial behavior
☐ 反社会性パーソナリティ障害	antisocial personality disorder
☐ 反射弓	reflex arc
☐ 反射特徴	reflectance characteristic
☐ 反証	falsification
☐ 反対色説	opponent-color theory
☐ 判断者間信頼性	interjudge reliability
☐ ハンチントン病	Huntington's disease
☐ 汎適応症候群	general adaptive syndrome, GAS
☐ パンデモニウム	pandemonium
☐ 反転計画法	reversal design
☐ 反動形成	reaction formation
☐ **反応**	**response**
☐ 反応間間隔	interresponse time, IRT
☐ **反応形成**	**shaping**
☐ 反応コスト	response cost
☐ **反応時間**	**reaction time**, **RT**; response time

☐ 反応性相互作用	reactive interaction
☐ 反応潜時	response latency
☐ 反応バイアス	response bias
☐ 反応妨害法	response prevention
☐ 反応ポテンシャル	reaction potential
☐ 反比例	inverse proportion
☐ 万魔殿	pandemonium
☐ 汎理論的モデル	transtheoretical model
☐ ピアソンの積率相関係数	Pearson's product-moment correlation coefficient
☐ PFスタディ	picture-frustration study, PF study
☐ PDPモデル	parallel distributed processing model
☐ 非学習性の行動	unlearned behavior
☐ **比較心理学**	**comparative psychology**
☐ 比較文化心理学	cross-cultural psychology
☐ **悲観主義**	**pessimism**
☐ ひきこもり	withdrawal
☐ 被虐待児症候群	buttered child syndrome
☐ ピグマリオン効果	Pygmalion effect
☐ 非言語的行動	nonverbal behavior
☐ 非言語的コミュニケーション	nonverbal communication
☐ 非現実的楽観主義	unrealistic optimism
☐ **被験者,被検者**	**subject**
☐ **被験者間計画**	**between-subject(s) design**
☐ 被験者間要因	between-subject(s) factor
☐ **被験者内計画**	**within-subject(s) design**
☐ 被験者内要因	within-subject(s) factor
☐ 被験者バイアス	subject bias
☐ 被験体	subject
☐ 非行	delinquency
☐ 非公式	informal
☐ 非公式集団	informal group

☐ 非公式な規範	informal norm
☐ 非構造化面接	unstructured interview
☐ 非合理な信念	irrational belief
☐ 微細脳損傷	minimal brain damage
☐ 非指示的	nondirective
☐ 非指示的カウンセリング	nondirective counseling
☐ 非指示的面接	nondirective interview
☐ 皮質	cortex
☐ 非実験法	nonexperimental method
☐ ヒステリー	hysteria
☐ 非ゼロ和ゲーム	non-zero-sum game
☐ 非線型	nonlinear
☐ ピック病	Pick's disease
☐ ビッグ・ファイブ	Big Five
☐ ヒット《信号検出理論の》	hit
☐ ヒット率《信号検出理論の》	hit rate
☐ 非定型抗精神病薬	atypical antipsychotics
☐ 否認	denial
☐ 疲憊期	stage of exhaustion
☐ 皮膚温	skin temperature
☐ 皮膚抵抗反応	skin resistance response, SRR
☐ 皮膚電位反応	skin potential response, SPR
☐ 皮膚電気活動	electrodermal activity, EDA
☐ 皮膚電気反射	electrodermal reflex
☐ 皮膚電気反応	galvanic skin response, GSR
☐ 皮膚伝導反応	skin conductance response, SCR
☐ 皮膚防衛システム	skin-defense system
☐ 疲弊期	stage of exhaustion
☐ 肥満	obesity
☐ 比喩	figurative language; metaphor
☐ ヒューマニスティック心理学	humanistic psychology
☐ ヒューマニスト	humanist
☐ **ヒューリスティック**	**heuristic**

☐ 表	table	
☐ 評価	evaluation; assessment	
☐ 評価懸念	evaluation apprehension	
☐ 病気行動	illness behavior	
☐ 表現型《生物の》	phenotype	
☐ 表示規則	display rule	
☐ 病者役割行動	sick-role behavior	
☐ 表出	expression	
☐ 標準	standard	
☐ **標準化**	**standardization**	
☐ 標準誤差	standard error (of the mean), SEM	
☐ 標準得点	standard score; z score	
☐ **標準偏差**	**standard deviation, SD**	
☐ **表象**	**representation**	
☐ **表情**	**facial expression**	
☐ 表象媒介過程	representational mediation process	
☐ 表層構造	surface structure	
☐ **表題**	**title**	
☐ 評定者間一致度	interrater agreement	
☐ 評定者間信頼性	interrater reliability	
☐ 評定尺度	rating scale	
☐ 標的オペラント	target operant	
☐ 標的刺激	target	
☐ **標本**	**sample**	
☐ 標本誤差	sampling error	
☐ **標本抽出**	**sampling**	
☐ 標本調査	sample survey	
☐ 表面的妥当性	face validity	
☐ 病理(学)	pathology	
☐ 開いた質問	opened question	
☐ 比率スケジュール	ratio schedule	
☐ 昼寝	nap, napping	
☐ 比例尺度	ratio scale	

☐ 非連合学習	nonassociative learning
☐ 疲労	fatigue
☐ 広場恐怖(症)	agoraphobia
☐ 敏感期	sensitive period
☐ 品種改良	selective breeding
☐ ファイ現象	phi-phenomenon
☐ ファセット	facet
☐ **不安**	**anxiety**
☐ 不安階層(表)	hierarchy of fear
☐ 不安症〔障害〕	anxiety disorder
☐ 不安の階層	anxiety hierarchy
☐ フィッシャーの正確〔直接〕確率検定	Fisher's exact test
☐ フィードバック	feedback
☐ VPI職業興味検査	Vocational Preference Inventory
☐ フィールド実験	field experiment
☐ 夫婦療法	marital therapy
☐ フェイスシート	face sheet
☐ フェヒナーの法則	Fechner's law
☐ フェロモン	pheromone
☐ 不応期	refractory period
☐ フォーカシング	focusing
☐ フォーマル	formal
☐ フォルス・アラーム《信号検出理論の》	false alarm, FA
☐ フォルス・アラーム率	false-alarms rate
☐ フォロワー	follower
☐ 孵化効果	incubation effect
☐ 賦活睡眠	activated sleep
☐ 不規則的睡眠	irregular sleep
☐ 不均衡状態	imbalance
☐ 復号化	decoding
☐ **副交感神経系**	**parasympathetic nervous system, PNS**

☐ 複合T迷路	multiple T-maze
☐ 複雑細胞	complex cell
☐ 腹式呼吸	abdominal breathing
☐ 服従	obedience
☐ 複数回答法	multiple answer
☐ 輻輳	convergence
☐ 輻輳開散運動	vergence movement
☐ 符号化	coding; encoding
☐ 符号化移行仮説	encoding-shift hypothesis
☐ 符号化段階	encoding stage
☐ 符号化特性原理	encoding specificity principle
☐ 不随意活動	involuntary activity
☐ 物質関連障害	substance-related disorder
☐ 物質主義	materialism
☐ フット・イン・ザ・ドア・テクニック	foot-in-the-door technique
☐ 物理学	physics
☐ 物理的記述	physical description
☐ 不適応行動	maladaptive behavior
☐ 不登校	school refusal
☐ 負の強化	negative reinforcement
☐ 負の相関関係	negative correlation
☐ 負の転移	negative transfer
☐ 負の罰	negative punishment
☐ 負のフィードバック	negative feedback
☐ 部分報告法	partial-report procedure
☐ 普遍性	universality
☐ 普遍的遅延モデル	general slowing model
☐ 不眠症	insomnia
☐ プライバシー	privacy
☐ プライバシーの権利	right to privacy
☐ **プライミング**	**priming**
☐ プライム	prime

☐ ブラインドテスト	blind technique (test)
☐ プラグマ	pragma
☐ プラグマティクス	pragmatics
☐ プラシーボ	placebo
☐ フラストレーション	frustration
☐ **プラセボ**	**placebo**
☐ プラセボ効果	placebo effect
☐ フラッシュバック	flashback
☐ フラッシュバルブ記憶	flashbulb memory
☐ フラッディング(法)	flooding
☐ プラトー現象	plateau
☐ フリーオペラント	free operant
☐ フリッカーテスト	flicker test
☐ プリテスト	pretest
☐ ブリーフセラピー	brief therapy
☐ プリマックの原理	Premack principle
☐ フリーライダー	free rider
☐ ふるえ	tremor
☐ プルキニエ現象	Purkinje phenomenon
☐ プレグナンツの法則	law of Prägnanz
☐ フロイト的言い間違い	Freudian slip
☐ ブローカ失語症	Broca's aphasia
☐ ブローカ野《運動性言語中枢》	Broca's area
☐ プロスペクト理論	prospect theory
☐ プロセス評価	process evaluation
☐ プロダクション	production
☐ フローチャート・モデル	flowchart model
☐ ブロッキング	blocking
☐ ブロックの法則	Bloch's law
☐ プロトコル	protocol
☐ プロトタイプ	prototype
☐ プローブ項目	probe item
☐ フロー理論	flow theory

☐ 分化	differentiation
☐ 分解	degradation
☐ 分化強化	differential reinforcement
☐ 文化心理学	cultural psychology
☐ 文化的に公平な知能検査	culture-fair intelligence test
☐ 文献研究	literature review
☐ **分散**	**variance**
☐ 分散学習	distributed learning; spaced learning
☐ **分散分析**	**analysis of variance, ANOVA**; variance analysis
☐ 分時心拍数	beats per minute, bpm
☐ 分子的〔微視的〕行動	molecular behavior
☐ 文章完成法	sentence completion test, SCT
☐ 分析的思考	analytic thought
☐ 文の真偽判断課題, 文判断課題	sentence verification task
☐ 分配的注意	divided attention
☐ 分泌	secretion
☐ 分布	distribution
☐ 文法	grammar
☐ 文法形態素	grammatical morpheme
☐ **文脈**	**context**
☐ 文脈依存効果	context dependency effect
☐ 文脈刺激	contextual stimuli
☐ 分離脳	split brain
☐ 分離不安	separation anxiety
☐ **平均(値)**	**mean**
☐ 平均順位	mean order
☐ 閉合	closure
☐ ベイズ統計学	Bayesian statistics
☐ 並列処理	parallel processing
☐ 並列分散処理モデル	parallel distributed processing model
☐ ベキ関数	power function

☐ ペシミズム	pessimism
☐ ベースライン	baseline
☐ ベータ波	β wave
☐ ベック抑うつ尺度	Beck Depression Inventory, BDI
☐ ヘッブの法則，ヘブ則	Hebbian rule
☐ ヘルスケアシステム	health care system
☐ ペルソナ	persona
☐ ヘルツ	hertz, Hz
☐ ヘロイン	heroin
☐ 辺縁系	limbic system
☐ 変化への抵抗	reactance
☐ 変換	transduction
☐ 変(動)間隔スケジュール	variable interval schedule
☐ 変形生成規則	transformational generative rule
☐ 変形生成文法	transformational generative grammar
☐ 偏見	prejudice
☐ 偏差	deviation
☐ 偏差値	T score
☐ 偏差知能指数	deviation IQ
☐ **変数**	**variable**
☐ ベンゾジアゼピン	benzodiazepines
☐ 扁桃体	amygdala
☐ 変(動)比率スケジュール	variable ratio schedule
☐ **弁別**	**discrimination**
☐ 弁別閾	difference [differential] threshold; difference [differential] limen
☐ 弁別刺激	discriminative stimulus
☐ 弁別性	distinctiveness
☐ 弁別反応時間	discrimination reaction time, DRT
☐ 変量効果	random effect
☐ **防衛機構，防衛機制**	**defense mechanism**
☐ 傍観者効果	bystander effect

☐ 忘却	**forgetting**
☐ 防御反射	defensive reflex
☐ **報酬**	**reward**
☐ 暴集	mob
☐ 報酬性の条件づけ	reward conditioning
☐ 報酬勢力	reward power
☐ 放心(状態)	absent-mindedness
☐ **方法**	**method**
☐ 飽満	satiation
☐ 方略	strategy
☐ 飽和	saturation
☐ 保持	retention
☐ ポジティブ心理学	positive psychology
☐ **母集団**	**population**
☐ 補償	compensation
☐ 補助仮説	auxiliary hypothesis
☐ 補色	complementary color
☐ 母数	parameter
☐ ポストテスト	posttest
☐ ホスピス	hospice
☐ ホスピタリズム	hospitalism
☐ 母性剥奪	maternal deprivation
☐ 保存	conservation
☐ ホーソン研究	Hawthorne research
☐ 没個性化	deindividuation
☐ ポップアウト	pop out
☐ **ボトムアップ処理**	**bottom-up processing**
☐ **ホメオスタシス**	**homeostasis**
☐ ポリアンナ仮説	Pollyanna hypothesis
☐ ポリグラフ	polygraph
☐ **ホルモン**	**hormone**
☐ ホン	phon
☐ **本能**	**instinct**

☐ 本能的逸脱	instinctive drift
☐ 本能的行動	instinctive behavior
☐ 本能的漂流	instinctive drift
☐ 本来感	authenticity

ま行

☐ マイノリティ	minority
☐ 前向き研究	prospective study
☐ マガーク効果	McGurk effect
☐ マガジン訓練	magazine training
☐ マグニチュード推定法	magnitude estimation
☐ マクノーテン裁定	M'Naghten Rule
☐ マジョリティ	majority
☐ マスキング	masking
☐ マスキング効果	masking effect
☐ マターナル・デプリベーション	maternal deprivation
☐ 末梢主義	peripheralism
☐ **末梢神経系**	**peripheral nervous system**
☐ マッハの帯, マッハバンド	Mach band
☐ まどろみ	drowsiness
☐ マニア	mania
☐ マネジリアル・グリッド	managerial grid
☐ まばたき	blink
☐ マリファナ	marijuana
☐ 蔓延	prevalence
☐ 慢性の	chronic
☐ マンセル表色系	Munsell system
☐ 満腹中枢	satiety center
☐ 味覚	gustation
☐ 味覚嫌悪学習	taste aversion learning
☐ 味受容器	taste receptor
☐ ミス《信号検出理論の》	miss

☐ ミスマッチ陰性電位	mismatch negativity, MMN
☐ **見通し**	**insight**
☐ ミニメンタル・ステート検査	Mini-Mental State Examination, MMSE
☐ ミネソタ多面的人格目録	Minnesota Multiphasic Personality Inventory, MMPI
☐ 脈波	pulse wave
☐ 脈拍伝達〔播〕時間〔速度〕	pulse transit time, PTT
☐ ミューラー・リヤー錯視	Müller-Lyer illusion
☐ **無意識**	**unconsciousness**
☐ 無意図的反応	involuntary response
☐ 無意味綴り	nonsense syllable
☐ 無関係性の学習	learned irrelevance
☐ 無関心期	precontemplation
☐ 無感動	apathy
☐ 無言症	mutism
☐ 無作為化	randomization
☐ 無作為化比較試験	randomized controlled trial, RCT
☐ **無作為抽出**	**random sampling**
☐ 無作為配分	random assignment
☐ 無作為標本	random sample
☐ **無作為割り当て**	**random assignment**
☐ **無条件刺激**	**unconditioned stimulus**, **US**; **UCS**
☐ 無条件の肯定的配慮	unconditional positive regard
☐ **無条件反射**	**unconditioned reflex**
☐ **無条件反応**	**unconditioned response**, **UR**; **UCR**
☐ 結びつけ問題	binding problem
☐ 無罰的反応	impunitive response
☐ 無名性	anonymity
☐ 名義尺度	nominal scale
☐ 明順応	light adaptation
☐ 明晰夢	lucid dream
☐ 瞑想	meditation

☐ 命題	proposition
☐ 命題記憶	propositional memory
☐ 命題的思考	propositional thought
☐ 明度	lightness; value
☐ メカニクス	mechanics
☐ メカニズム	mechanism
☐ メタコントラスト	metacontrast
☐ メタドン	methadone
☐ メタ認知	metacognition
☐ メタファー	metaphor
☐ メタ分析	meta analysis
☐ メラトニン	melatonin
☐ メル尺度	mel scale
☐ 免疫	immune
☐ 免疫系	immune system
☐ **面接**	**interview**
☐ 面接法	interview technique
☐ メンタルモデル	mental model
☐ メンバー	member
☐ 盲検法	blind technique (test)
☐ 妄想	delusion
☐ 妄想型	paranoid
☐ 網膜	retina
☐ 網膜視床下部路	retino-hypothalamic tract
☐ 網様体	reticular formation
☐ 燃え尽き	burnout
☐ モーガンの公準	Morgan's canon
☐ 目撃証言	eyewitness testimony
☐ 目的的行動	purposive behavior
☐ 目標	goal
☐ 目標づけられた思考，目標的思考	directed thinking
☐ 目標づけられない思考	undirected thinking

☐ 目録	inventory
☐ モーズレー人格目録	Maudsley Personality Inventory, MPI
☐ モダリティ	modality
☐ **モデリング**	**modeling**
☐ モノアミン酸化酵素	monoamine oxidase, MAO
☐ 物語文法	story grammar
☐ ものの永続性	object permanence
☐ 模倣	imitation
☐ モラトリアム	moratorium
☐ モラール	morale
☐ モロー反射	Moro reflex
☐ **問題解決**	**problem solving**
☐ 問題解決スキル	problem-solving skill
☐ 問題空間	problem space
☐ 問題焦点型コーピング	problem-focused coping
☐ 問題箱	problem box; puzzle box

や 行

☐ ヤーキーズ゠ダッドソンの法則	Yerkes-Dodson law
☐ 薬物依存	drug dependence
☐ 薬物乱用	drug abuse
☐ **役割**	**role**
☐ 役割固定法	fixed role therapy
☐ 役割スキーマ	role schema
☐ 役割喪失	role loss
☐ 野性児	feral child
☐ 友愛	companionate love
☐ 有意差	significant difference
☐ 有意水準	level of significance; significant level

☐ 誘意性	valence
☐ (統計的に)有意な	**significant**
☐ 誘因	**incentive**
☐ 誘因動機づけ	incentive motivation
☐ 有益刺激への接近学習	approach learning
☐ 有機体	organism
☐ 遊戯療法	play therapy
☐ 優生学	eugenics
☐ 郵送調査	mail survey
☐ 誘導	induction
☐ 誘導運動	induced motion
☐ 誘導質問, 誘導尋問	leading question
☐ 誘発電位	evoked potential, EP
☐ 有病率	prevalence
☐ 有毛細胞	hair cells
☐ 猶予期間	moratorium
☐ 床効果	floor effect
☐ 夢分析	dream analysis
☐ 葉《脳などの》	lobe
☐ 要因	**factor**
☐ 要因計画	factorial design
☐ 要求	demand; need
☐ 要求水準	level of aspiration
☐ 要求特性	demand characteristics
☐ 幼児	**infant**
☐ 幼児期	**infancy**; early childhood
☐ 幼児期健忘	childhood amnesia
☐ 陽性症状	positive symptom
☐ 陽性の幻覚	positive hallucination
☐ 容積脈波	plethysmogram
☐ 要素主義	elementalism
☐ 陽電子放射断層撮影	positron emission tomography, PET

☐ 要約	**abstract; summary**
☐ 予期	expectation
☐ 予期説	expectancy theory
☐ 予期的反応	anticipatory response
☐ 抑圧	repression
☐ **抑うつ**	**depression**
☐ 抑うつ障害	depressive disorder
☐ **抑制**	**inhibition**
☐ 抑制子	inhibitor
☐ 抑制条件づけ	inhibitory conditioning
☐ 抑制性結合	inhibitory connections
☐ 抑制薬	depressants
☐ 抑制率	suppression ratio, SR
☐ 欲動	instinct
☐ **欲望**	**desire**
☐ 横軸	horizontal axis
☐ **予測**	**prediction**
☐ 予測可能性	predictability
☐ 予測的妥当性	predictive validity
☐ **欲求**	**need**
☐ 欲求階層説	hierarchy of needs
☐ **欲求不満**	**frustration**
☐ 欲求不満攻撃仮説	frustration-aggression hypothesis
☐ 欲求不満耐性	frustration tolerance
☐ 予備研究	pilot study
☐ 予備調査	pretest
☐ 予防	prevention
☐ 予防的健康行動	health protective behavior; preventive health behavior
☐ 世論調査	poll
☐ 四体液説	humorism

ら行

☐ **来談者**	**client**
☐ **来談者中心療法**	**client centered therapy**
☐ ライフイベント	life event
☐ ライフヒストリー研究	study of life history
☐ 楽観主義	optimism
☐ ラベリング効果	labeling effect
☐ **ラポール**	**rapport**
☐ ラムダ反応	lambda response
☐ ラムダ〔λ〕複合	lambda complex
☐ 乱数	random numbers
☐ ランダムサンプリング	random sampling
☐ ランダムドット・ステレオグラム	random dot stereogram, RDS
☐ リアクタンス	reactance
☐ リアリティ・オリエンテーション	reality orientation , RO
☐ リアリティ・モニタリング	reality monitoring
☐ 理解	comprehension
☐ 理学療法士	physical therapist, PT
☐ 力学的制御理論	dynamic control theory
☐ 力動的心理療法	dynamic psychotherapy
☐ 離散試行	discrete trial
☐ リスクファクター	risk factor
☐ リズム	rhythm
☐ リーダー	leader
☐ リーダーシップ	leadership
☐ 利他性	altruism
☐ 離脱	withdrawal
☐ 離脱症状	withdrawal symptoms
☐ リーチング	reaching
☐ リッカート法	Likert scaling
☐ 律動	rhythm

☐	リテラシー	literacy
☐	利得行列	pay-off matrix
☐	**リハーサル**	**rehearsal**
☐	リビドー	libido
☐	リビングウィル	living will
☐	リボ核酸	ribonucleic acid, RNA
☐	流言	rumor
☐	流行	fashion; prevalence
☐	流動性知能	fluid intelligence
☐	領域	domain
☐	両価性	ambivalence
☐	良識	sense
☐	利用可能性	availability
☐	利用可能性ヒューリスティック	availability heuristic
☐	両側検定	two-tailed test
☐	両眼視差	binocular parallax; binocular disparity
☐	両義性	ambivalence
☐	両耳分離聴	dichotic listening
☐	両性具有, 両性	androgyny
☐	両側性転移	bilateral transfer
☐	**量的変数**	**quantitative variable**
☐	量の保存	conservation of quantity
☐	**リラクセーション**	**relaxation**
☐	**理論**	**theory**
☐	臨界閾	critical region
☐	**臨界期**	**critical period**
☐	臨界フリッカー周波数	critical flicker frequency, CFF
☐	**臨床心理学**	**clinical psychology**
☐	臨床心理学者, 臨床心理士	clinical psychologist
☐	**倫理(学)**	**ethics**
☐	倫理基準	ethical standards
☐	**類型**	**type**

☐ 類型論	typology
☐ 類似(性)	similarity
☐ 類似性ヒューリスティック	similarity heuristic
☐ 類推	analogy
☐ 類同	similarity
☐ 類同による群化	grouping by similarity
☐ 霊能力者	psychic
☐ 霊能力	psychic power
☐ レジリエンス	resilience
☐ レスコーラ゠ワグナー・モデル	Rescorla-Wagner model
☐ レスポンデント	respondent
☐ レスポンデント条件づけ	respondent conditioning
☐ レセプター	receptor
☐ 劣等感	inferiority
☐ レディネス	readiness
☐ レミニセンス	reminiscence
☐ レム周期	REM cycle
☐ **レム睡眠**	**rapid eye movement sleep, REM sleep**
☐ 恋愛の三要素説	triangular theory of love
☐ **連合**	**association**
☐ 連合学習	associative learning
☐ 連合強度	associative strength
☐ 連合弛緩	loosening of associations
☐ 連合主義	associationism
☐ 連合主義心理学	associationist psychology
☐ 連合野	associative area
☐ 連鎖反射	chain reflex
☐ 練習	practice
☐ 練習効果	practice effect
☐ 連続強化	continuous reinforcement
☐ 連続体モデル	continuum model
☐ 連動統制法	yoked control technique

☐ 老人用うつスケール	geriatric depression scale, GDS
☐ 老年学	gerontology
☐ 老年期	senescence
☐ ロゴテラピー	logotherapy
☐ ローデータ	raw data
☐ ロボトミー	lobotomy
☐ ロー・ボール・テクニック	low-ball technique
☐ ロールシャッハ検査, ロールシャッハ・テスト	Rorschach Test
☐ ロールプレイング	role playing
☐ 論議	discussion
☐ 論理	logic
☐ 論理情動行動療法	rational emotive behavior therapy, REBT
☐ 論理療法	rational therapy

わ行

☐ ワーキングメモリー	working memory
☐ ワーディング	wording

人名集

欧文表記	カタカナ表記	生年
Adler, Alfred 個人心理学,劣等感	アドラー, A.	1870
Ainsworth, Mary D. S. ストレンジ・シチュエーション法	エインズワース, M. D. S.	1913
Allport, Gordon W. 人格心理学,流言研究	オールポート, G. W.	1897
Angell, James R. 機能主義	エンジェル, J. R	1869
Aristotle ギリシャの哲学者,プラトン学派,精神論	アリストテレス	B. C. 384
Aronson, Elliot 応用社会心理学,対人魅力のゲイン・ロス効果	アロンソン, E.	1932
Asch, Solomon E. 実験社会心理学,同調	アッシュ, S. E.	1907
Atkinson, Richard C. 記憶の二重貯蔵モデル,短期記憶,長期記憶	アトキンソン, R. C.	1929
Baddeley, Alan D. ワーキングメモリー,作動記憶	バドリー, A. D.	1934
Baldwin, James M. こどもの進化論的発達,ボールドウィン効果	ボールドウィン, J. M.	1861
Bandura, Albert 社会的学習理論,モデリング	バンデューラ, A.	1925
Bartlett, Frederic C. 日常記憶,思考心理学	バートレット, F. C.	1886
Beck, Aaron T. うつ病の認知療法	ベック, A. T.	1921
Beers, Clifford W. 精神衛生,『わが魂に出会うまで』	ビアーズ, C. W.	1876
Békésy, Georg von 内耳蝸牛の研究,聴覚細胞の周波数対応	ベケシー, G. von	1899
Bem, Daryl J. 超感覚的知覚,自己知覚理論	ベム, D. J.	1938

Berger, Hans 脳波の記録，アルファ派の発見	ベルガー, H.	1873
Berkeley, George 英国経験論哲学，連合心理学の先駆	バークリー, G.	1685
Berne, Eric 交流分析	バーン, E.	1910
Binet, Alfred 知能研究，ビネー式知能検査	ビネー, A.	1857
Boring, Edwin G. 実験心理学史，感覚知覚研究	ボーリング, E. G.	1886
Bower, Gordon H. 気分一致効果，感情ネットワーク理論	バウワー, G. H.	1932
Bowlby, John 愛着理論，マターナル・デプリベーション理論	ボウルビィ, J.	1907
Brentano, Franz 作用心理学	ブレンターノ, F.	1838
Bridgman, Percy W. 物理学者，科学哲学，操作的定義	ブリッジマン, P. W.	1882
Broadbent, Donald E. 情報処理過程，注意のフィルターモデル，意思決定	ブロードベント, D. E.	1926
Broca, Paul ブローカ野，運動性言語中枢	ブローカ, P.	1824
Bruner, Jerome S. ニュールック心理学，認知発達	ブルーナー, J. S.	1915
Brunswik, Egon 知覚，レンズ・モデル	ブランズウィック, E.	1903
Byrne, Donn E. 対人魅力	バーン, D. E.	1931
Cacioppo, John T. 社会的認知神経科学	カシオッポ, J. T.	1951
Campbell, Donald T. 準実験計画，内的/外的妥当性	キャンベル, D. T.	1916

Cannon, Walter B. 生理学者，ホメオスタシス，キャノン=バード説	キャノン，W. B.	1871
Cattell, James M. 反応時間，個人差	キャッテル，J. M.	1860
Cattell, Raymond B. 特性論，16特性因子別性格検査，知能	キャッテル，R. B.	1905
Chomsky, Noam 変形生成文法，言語獲得装置	チョムスキー，N.	1928
Cialdini, Robert B. 社会的影響，説得のテクニック	チャルディーニ，R. B.	1945
Collins, Allan M. 意味記憶，ネットワーク・モデル，人工知能	コリンズ，A. M.	1937
Craik, Fergus I. M. 記憶の処理水準モデル	クレーク，F. I. M.	1935
Cronbach, Lee J. 信頼性理論，α係数	クロンバック，L. J.	1916
Darwin, Charles R. 進化論，『種の起源』	ダーウィン，C. R.	1809
Dawkins, Richard 利己的な遺伝子	ドーキンス，R.	1941
Deci, Edward L. 内発の動機づけ，認知的評価理論	デシ，E. L.	1942
Descartes René 方法的懐疑，心身二元論，反射	デカルト，R.	1596
Dewey, John プラグマティズム，機能主義	デューイ，J.	1859
Dodson, John D. 覚醒水準，ヤーキーズ=ダッドソンの法則	ダッドソン，J. D.	1879
Donders, Franciscus C. 減算法	ドンダース，F. C.	1818
Ebbinghaus, Hermann 記憶の実験研究，忘却曲線	エビングハウス，H.	1850

Eibl-Eibesfeldt, Irenäus	アイブル-アイベスフェルト, I.	1928
ヒューマン・エソロジー，動物行動学者，行動生態学		
Ekman, Paul	エクマン, P.	1934
表情，感情		
Ellis, Albert	エリス, A.	1913
論理療法，論理情動行動療法		
Emmert, Emil	エンメルト, E.	1844
残像効果，エンメルトの法則		
Erikson, Erik H.	エリクソン, E. H.	1902
自我同一性，人格発達研究		
Estes, William K.	エステス, W. K.	1919
刺激抽出理論，条件性情動反応		
Eysenck, Hans J.	アイゼンク, H. J.	1916
行動療法，モーズレイ人格検査		
Fechner, Gustav T.	フェヒナー, G. T.	1801
精神物理学，フェヒナーの法則		
Festinger, Leon	フェスティンガー, L.	1919
認知的不協和，社会的比較過程		
Fisher, Ronald A.	フィッシャー, R. A.	1890
実験計画，統計，F検定		
Frankl, Viktor E.	フランクル, V. E.	1905
実存分析，ロゴテラピー，『夜と霧』		
Freud, Anna	フロイト, A.	1895
新フロイト派，児童臨床，自我心理学		
Freud, Sigmund	フロイト, S.	1856
精神分析学，エディプス・コンプレックス		
Fromm, Erich	フロム, E.	1900
新フロイト派，『自由からの逃走』		
Galenus	ガレノス	129
脳室機能局在説，精神の気		
Gall, Franz J.	ガル, F. J.	1757
骨相学		

人名（英→和） C〜G

Galton, Francis 遺伝研究，優生学，相関，共感覚	ゴールトン, F.	1822
Galvani, Luigi 生理学者，電気活動による神経伝達	ガルバーニ, L.	1737
Gardner, Howard E. 多重知能理論	ガードナー, H. E.	1943
Gazzaniga, Michael S. 分離脳	ガザニガ, M. S.	1939
Gesell, Arnold. L. 双生児統制法，成熟優位説	ゲゼル, A. L.	1880
Gibson, Eleanor J. 奥行き知覚，視覚的断崖	ギブソン, E. J.	1910
Gibson, James J. 生態学的知覚，生態光学，アフォーダンス	ギブソン, J. J.	1904
Goddard, Henry H. 優生学，犯罪，知能，遺伝	ゴダード, H. H.	1866
Goleman, Daniel J. 情動知能	ゴールマン, D. J.	1946
Golgi, Camillo ゴルジ染色	ゴルジ, C.	1843
Guilford, Joy P. 精神測定法，知能の構造模型，性格検査	ギルフォード, J. P.	1897
Guthrie, Edwin R. 学習，連合，刺激と反応の時間空間的接近理論	ガスリー, E. R.	1886
Guttman, Louis 態度測定，ガットマンの尺度分析法	ガットマン, L.	1916
Hall, Granville S. 米国心理学初代会長，米国初の心理学実験室	ホール, G. S.	1844
Harlow, Harry F. 代理母実験，学習セット	ハーロー, H. F.	1905
Hebb, Donald O. 細胞集成体，ヘブ則，感覚遮断	ヘッブ, D. O.	1904

Heider, Fritz	ハイダー, F.	1896
社会心理学，帰属，態度のバランス理論		
Helmholtz, Hermann L. F. von	ヘルムホルツ, H. L. F. von	1821
ヤング＝ヘルムホルツの三色説，聴覚の共鳴説，神経刺激伝導の測定		
Hering, Heinrich E.	ヘリング, H. E.	1834
感覚生理学，色覚の反対色説，空間知覚説		
Higgins, Tory E.	ヒギンズ, T. E.	1946
自己不一致理論		
Hilgard, Ernest R.	ヒルガード, E. R.	1904
学習，条件づけ，催眠，ペイン・コントロール		
Hippocrates	ヒポクラテス	B.C.460
医学の祖，四体液説		
Holmes, Thomas H.	ホームズ, T. H.	1918
ストレス，社会的再適応評定尺度		
Horney, Karen	ホーナイ, K.	1885
新フロイト派，社会文化的精神分析学		
Hubel, David H.	ヒューベル, D. H.	1926
視覚神経生理学，大脳皮質における感覚情報処理		
Hull, Clark L.	ハル, C. L.	1884
習慣強度と動因，『行動の原理』		
Hume, David	ヒューム, D.	1711
英国経験論，連合心理学の先駆，人間は「知覚の束」		
James, William	ジェームズ, W.	1842
機能主義，意識の流れ，ジェームズ＝ランゲ説		
Janet, Pierre M. F.	ジャネ, P. M. F.	1859
神経症，ヒステリー症状		
Janis, Irving L.	ジャニス, I. L.	1918
集団思考		
Johnson-Laird, Philip N.	ジョンソン-レアード, P. N.	1936
認知心理学，メンタルモデル		
Jung, Carl G.	ユング, C. G.	1875
分析心理学，集合的無意識，内向・外向		

人名（英→和）　G〜J

Kagan, Jerome 　発達心理学，気質	ケイガン，J.	1929
Kahneman, Daniel 　意思決定，プロスペクト理論，行動経済学	カーネマン，D.	1934
Kandel, Eric R. 　神経生理学，神経系の情報伝達	カンデル，E. R.	1929
Kanizsa, Gaetano 　ゲシュタルト心理学，主観的輪郭	カニッツァ，G.	1913
Kanner, Leo 　自閉症	カナー，L.	1894
Kelley, Harold H. 　原因帰属の分散分析モデル	ケリー，H. H.	1921
Kelly, George A. 　パーソナル・コンストラクト理論	ケリー，G. A.	1905
Klein, Melanie 　新フロイト派，対象関係論	クライン，M.	1882
Koffka, Kurt 　『ゲシュタルト心理学の原理』	コフカ，K.	1886
Kohlberg, Lawrence 　道徳性発達理論	コールバーグ，L.	1927
Köhler, Wolfgang 　ゲシュタルト，洞察，移調	ケーラー，W.	1887
Konorski, Jerzy 　神経生理学，生理心理学，条件反射	コノルスキ，J.	1903
Kosslyn, Stephen M. 　心的回転，心的イメージ走査実験	コスリン，S. M.	1948
Kraepelin, Emil 　近代精神医学の父，精神作業検査法	クレペリン，E.	1856
Kretschmer, Ernst 　精神病理学，類型論，体型説	クレッチマー，E.	1888
Lacan, Jacques M. É. 　新フロイト派，構造主義，鏡像段階	ラカン，J. M. É.	1901

Lange, Carl G.	ランゲ, C. G.	1834
情動理論, ジェームズ=ランゲ説		
Lashley, Karl S.	ラシュレー, K. S.	1890
実験神経心理学, 等能性の原理, 量作用の原理		
Latané, Bibb	ラタネ, B.	1937
社会的手抜き		
Lazarus, Richard S.	ラザルス, R. S.	1922
認知的評価理論, ストレス・コーピング理論		
Lewin, Kurt Z.	レヴィン, K. Z.	1890
場の理論, 集団力学, アクションリサーチ		
Likert, Rensis	リッカート, R.	1903
態度測定, リッカート法		
Locke, John	ロック, J.	1632
英国経験論, タブラ・ラサ		
Lockhart, Robert S.	ロックハート, R. S.	1939
記憶の処理水準モデル		
Loeb, Jacques	ローブ, J.	1859
刺激相称, 動物の相性研究		
Loftus, Elizabeth F.	ロフタス, E. F.	1944
目撃証言, 虚偽記憶		
Lorenz, Konrad Z.	ローレンツ, K. Z.	1903
動物行動学, 刻印づけ, 刷り込み		
Luria, Alexander R.	ルリア, A. R.	1902
力動的局在論, 神経心理学的検査, 戦時脳損傷研究, 失語症		
MacLean, Paul D.	マクリーン, P. D.	1913
三位一体脳, 反射脳, 情動脳, 理性脳		
Maslow, Abraham H.	マズロー, A. H.	1908
欲求階層説, 人間性心理学		
McClelland, David C.	マクレランド, D. C.	1917
達成動機, コンピテンス		
McClelland, James L.	マクレランド, J. L.	1948
ニューラルネットワーク, 並列分散処理モデル		

McGuire, William J. 説得への抵抗,接種理論	マグガイア, W. J.	1925
Mead, George H. 自己論,主我と客我	ミード, G. H.	1863
Meichenbaum, Donald H. 認知行動療法,自己教示訓練,ストレス免疫訓練	マイケンバウム, D. H.	1940
Melzack, Ronald 痛みのゲートコントロール理論,幻肢痛	メルザック, R.	1929
Milgram, Stanley 権威への服従,スモール・ワールド現象	ミルグラム, S.	1933
Mill, John S. 心的化学,『自由論』,『功利論』	ミル, J. S.	1806
Miller, George A. 短期記憶,マジカルナンバー7	ミラー, G. A.	1920
Miller, Neal E. 回避行動,模倣行動,バイオフィードバック	ミラー, N. E.	1909
Minsky, Marvin L. 人工知能,パーセプトロン,『心の社会』	ミンスキー, M. L.	1927
Moreno, Jacob L. ソシオメトリー	モレノ, J. L.	1892
Morgan, Lloyd 比較心理学,モーガンの公準	モーガン, L.	1852
Mowrer, Orval H. 学習の二要因理論,媒介過程説	マウラー, O. H.	1907
Münsterberg, Hugo 応用心理学,精神工学	ミュンスターバーグ, H.	1863
Murray, Henry A. 社会的動機,主題統覚検査	マレー, H. A.	1893
Neisser, Ulric 認知心理学	ナイサー, U.	1928
Newcomb, Theodore M. 社会規範,態度	ニューカム, T. M.	1903

Newell, Allen 人工知能	ニューウェル, A.	1927
Norman, Donald A. 情報処理心理学, インターフェース, ユーザビリティ	ノーマン, D. A.	1935
Olds, James 脳内自己刺激, 快楽中枢	オールズ, J.	1922
Osgood, Charles E. SD法, ポリアンナ効果, 表象媒介過程	オズグッド, C. E.	1916
Paivio, Allan U. 二重符号化仮説, イメージ・アナログ説	ペイビオ, A. U.	1925
Pavlov, Ivan P. 古典的条件づけ, 条件反射	パブロフ, I. P.	1849
Pearson, Karl 生物測定学, 積率相関係数	ピアソン, K.	1857
Penfield, Wilder G. ペンフィールドの脳地図, 脳の機能局在	ペンフィールド, W. G.	1891
Perls, Frederick S. ゲシュタルト療法	パールズ, F. S.	1893
Piaget, Jean 認知発達段階, 発生的認識論, 知能・道徳性の発達	ピアジェ, J.	1896
Plato イデア論, 心身二元論	プラトン	B.C.427
Portmann, Adolf 生理的早産	ポルトマン, A.	1897
Posner, Michael I. 先行手がかり法, 注意のスポットライト説	ポズナー, M. I.	1936
Premack, David 心の理論	プレマック, D.	1925
Plutchik, Robert 感情の環, 感情立体モデル	プルチック, R.	1927
Pylyshyn, Zenon W. 視覚的注意, 多物体追跡, 心的イメージ	ピリシン, Z. W.	1937

Rahe, Richard H. ストレス，社会的再適応評定尺度	ラーエ，R. H.	1936
Ramón y Cajal, Santiago ニューロン説	ラモン=イ=カハール，S.	1852
Rescorla, Robert A. 古典的条件づけ，レスコーラ=ワグナー・モデル	レスコーラ，R. A.	1940
Rogers, Carl R. 来談者中心療法，非指示的カウンセリング，エンカウンター・グループ	ロジャーズ，C. R.	1902
Romanes, George J. 逸話法による動物心理研究	ロマネス，G. J.	1848
Rorschach, Hermann ロールシャッハ・テスト，投映法	ロールシャッハ，H.	1884
Rosch, Eleanor H. プロトタイプ理論，カテゴリ認知	ロッシュ，E. H.	1938
Rosenblatt, Frank パーセプトロン	ローゼンブラット，F.	1928
Rosenhan, David L. 精神疾患診断の実験	ローゼンハン，D. L.	1929
Rosenthal, Robert ピグマリオン効果	ローゼンタール，R.	1933
Rosenzweig, Mark R. 環境と大脳皮質の発達	ローゼンツワイク，M. R.	1922
Rotter, Julian B. 統制の所在，原因帰属	ロッター，J. B.	1916
Rubin, Edgar J. 図と地，ルビンの壺	ルビン，E. J.	1886
Rumelhart, David E. ニューラルネットワーク，並列分散処理	ラメルハート，D. E.	1942
Russell, James A. 感情の二次元円環モデル	ラッセル，J. A.	1947
Sapir, Edward サピア=ウォーフの仮説，言語相対性仮説	サピア，E.	1884

Saussure, Ferdinand de 近代言語学の父，記号論の基礎	ソシュール, F.	1857
Schachter, Stanley 情動二要因説，不安，親和仮説	シャクター, S.	1922
Schlosberg, Harold H. 感情の円環モデル	シュロスバーグ, H. H.	1904
Seligman, Martin E. P. 学習性無力感，ポジティブ心理学，オプティミズム研究	セリグマン, M. E. P.	1942
Selye, Hans ストレス，汎適応症候群	セリエ, H.	1907
Shannon, Claude E. 情報理論	シャノン, C. E.	1916
Sheldon, William H. 胚葉に基づく類型論，体型説	シェルドン, W. H.	1898
Shepard, Roger N. 心的回転	シェパード, R. N.	1929
Sherif, Muzafer 同調行動，集団規範	シェリフ, M.	1906
Sherrington, Charles S. 神経生理学，反射学，感覚生理学	シェリントン, C. S.	1857
Shiffrin, Richard M. 記憶の二重貯蔵モデル，短期記憶，長期記憶	シフリン, R. M.	1942
Simon, Herbert A. 意思決定理論，人工知能	サイモン, H. A.	1916
Skinner, Burrhus F. 徹底的行動主義，行動分析学，オペラント条件づけ	スキナー, B. F.	1904
Socrates 古代哲学，無知の知，ソクラテス式問答法	ソクラテス	B.C.469
Sokolov, Evgeny N. 定位反射，馴化	ソコロフ, E. N.	1920
Spalding, Douglas A. 刷り込み，子の刻印づけ	スポルディング, D. A.	1841

Spearman, Charles E. 知能の二因子説,順位相関係数	スピアマン,C. E.	1863
Spence, Kenneth W. 誘因動機づけ,移調の行動主義的分析	スペンス,K. W.	1907
Spencer, Herbert 社会進化論,適者生存	スペンサー,H.	1820
Sperling, George 感覚記憶,画像記憶,アイコニックメモリー	スパーリング,G.	1934
Sperry, Roger W. 分離脳,大脳半球の機能差	スペリー,R. W.	1913
Spielberger, Charles D. 状態−特性不安尺度	スピルバーガー,C. D.	1927
Spitz, René A. ホスピタリズム	スピッツ,R. A.	1887
Spranger, Eduard 価値志向に基づく類型論	シュプランガー,E.	1882
Squire, Larry R. 宣言的記憶	スクワイア,L. R.	1941
Stern, Louis W. 知能指数,輻輳説	スターン,L. W.	1871
Sternberg, Robert J. 知能の三部理論	スタンバーグ,R. J.	1949
Sternberg, Saul スタンバーグ記憶走査課題,加算要因法	スタンバーグ,S.	1933
Stevens, Stanley S. 尺度水準,べき法則	スティーヴンス,S. S.	1906
Sullivan, Harry S. 新フロイト派,対人関係論,関与しながらの観察	サリヴァン,H. S.	1892
Terman, Lewis M. 知能検査,ギフテッド研究	ターマン,L. M.	1877
Thorndike, Edward L. 効果の法則,問題箱実験,教育心理学	ソーンダイク,E. L.	1874

Thurstone, Louis L. 比較判断の法則，知能の多因子説	サーストン，L. L.	1887
Tinbergen, Nikolaas 動物行動学，解発刺激，4つの「なぜ」	ティンバーゲン，N.	1907
Titchener, Edward B. 構成心理学，内観による意識内容の分析	ティチェナー，E. B.	1867
Tolman, Edward C. 目的的行動主義，認知地図，潜在学習	トールマン，E. C.	1886
Tomkins, Silvan S. 生得的基本情動，感情の顔面フィードバック説	トムキンス，S. S.	1911
Treisman, Anne M. 特徴統合理論，視覚探索	トリーズマン，A. M.	1935
Triplett, Norman 社会的促進	トリプレット，N.	1861
Tulving, Endel エピソード記憶，意味記憶，符号化特性原理	タルヴィング，E.	1927
Tversky, Amos 意思決定，プロスペクト理論，認知バイアス	トヴァスキー，A.	1937
Vygotsky, Lev S. 発達の最近接領域，外言，内言	ヴィゴツキー，L. S.	1896
Wagner, Alan R. レスコーラ＝ワグナー・モデル	ワグナー，A. R.	1934
Wason, Peter C. 確証バイアス，4枚カード問題	ウェイソン，P. C.	1924
Watson, John B. 行動主義宣言，アルバート坊やの実験	ワトソン，J. B.	1878
Weber, Ernst H. ウェーバーの法則，弁別閾，触二点閾	ウェーバー，E. H.	1795
Wechsler, David ウェクスラー式知能検査	ウェクスラー，D.	1896
Weiner, Bernard 成功と失敗の原因帰属	ワイナー，B.	1935

Wernicke, Carl 　ウェルニッケ野，感覚性言語中枢	ウェルニッケ, C.	1848
Wertheimer, Max 　ゲシュタルト，プレグナンツの法則，生産的思考	ウェルトハイマー, M.	1880
Whorf, Benjamin L. 　サピア＝ウォーフの仮説，言語相対性仮説	ウォーフ, B. L.	1897
Wiener, Norbert 　サイバネティックス	ウィーナー, N.	1894
Wiesel, Torsten N. 　視覚神経生理学，単純細胞，複雑細胞	ウィーセル, T. N.	1924
Winnicott, Donald W. 　新フロイト派，移行対象，ホールディング	ウィニコット, D. W.	1896
Witmer, Lightner 　臨床心理学の父，世界初の心理クリニック	ウィトマー, L.	1867
Wolpe, Joseph 　系統的脱感作法，不安階層表，逆制止	ウォルピ, J.	1915
Woodworth, Robert S. 　動因，世界初の質問紙検査法	ウッドワース, R. S.	1869
Wundt, Wilhelm M. 　心理学の父，世界初の心理学実験室	ヴント, W. M.	1832
Yerkes, Robert M. 　ヤーキーズ＝ダッドソンの法則，霊長類研究，集団式知能検査	ヤーキーズ, R. M.	1876
Young, Thomas 　ヤング＝ヘルムホルツの三色説，光の波動説，光の干渉現象	ヤング, T.	1773
Zajonc, Robert B. 　単純接触効果，社会的促進	ザイアンス, R. B.	1923
Zimbardo, Philip G. 　没個性化，スタンフォード監獄実験	ジンバルドー, P. G.	1933

カタカナ表記	欧文表記	生年
アイゼンク, H. J. 行動療法，モーズレイ人格検査	Eysenck, Hans J.	1916
アイブル-アイベスフェルト, I. ヒューマン・エソロジー，動物行動学者，行動生態学	Eibl-Eibesfeldt, Irenäus	1928
アッシュ, S. E. 実験社会心理学，同調	Asch, Solomon E.	1907
アトキンソン, R. C. 記憶の二重貯蔵モデル，短期記憶，長期記憶	Atkinson, Richard C.	1929
アドラー, A. 個人心理学，劣等感	Adler, Alfred	1870
アリストテレス ギリシャの哲学者，プラトン学派，精神論	Aristotle	B. C. 384
アロンソン, E. 応用社会心理学，対人魅力のゲイン・ロス効果	Aronson, Elliot	1932
ヴィゴツキー, L. S. 発達の最近接領域，外言，内言	Vygotsky, Lev S.	1896
ウィーセル, T. N. 視覚神経生理学，単純細胞，複雑細胞	Wiesel, Torsten N.	1924
ウィトマー, L. 臨床心理学の父，世界初の心理クリニック	Witmer, Lightner	1867
ウィーナー, N. サイバネティックス	Wiener, Norbert	1894
ウィニコット, D. W. 新フロイト派，移行対象，ホールディング	Winnicott, Donald W.	1896
ウェイソン, P. C. 確証バイアス，4枚カード問題	Wason, Peter C.	1924
ウェクスラー, D. ウェクスラー式知能検査	Wechsler, David	1896
ウェーバー, E. H. ウェーバーの法則，弁別閾，触二点閾	Weber, Ernst H.	1795
ウェルトハイマー, M. ゲシュタルト，プレグナンツの法則，生産的思考	Wertheimer, Max	1880

ウェルニッケ, C. 　ウェルニッケ野，感覚性言語中枢	Wernicke, Carl	1848
ウォーフ, B. L. 　サピア=ウォーフの仮説，言語相対性仮説	Whorf, Benjamin L.	1897
ウォルピ, J. 　系統的脱感作法，不安階層表，逆制止	Wolpe, Joseph	1915
ウッドワース, R. S. 　動因，世界初の質問紙検査法	Woodworth, Robert S.	1869
ヴント, W. M. 　心理学の父，世界初の心理学実験室	Wundt, Wilhelm M.	1832
エインズワース, M. D. S. 　ストレンジ・シチュエーション法	Ainsworth, Mary D. S.	1913
エクマン, P. 　表情，感情	Ekman, Paul	1934
エステス, W. K. 　刺激抽出理論，条件性情動反応	Estes, William K.	1919
エビングハウス, H. 　記憶の実験研究，忘却曲線	Ebbinghaus, Hermann	1850
エリクソン, E. H. 　自我同一性，人格発達研究	Erikson, Erik H.	1902
エリス, A. 　論理療法，論理情動行動療法	Ellis, Albert	1913
エンジェル, J. R 　機能主義	Angell, James R.	1869
エンメルト, E. 　残像効果，エンメルトの法則	Emmert, Emil	1844
オズグッド, C. E. 　SD法，ポリアンナ効果，表象媒介過程	Osgood, Charles E.	1916
オールズ, J. 　脳内自己刺激，快楽中枢	Olds, James	1922
オールポート, G. W. 　人格心理学，流言研究	Allport, Gordon W.	1897

ガザニガ, M. S.	Gazzaniga, Michael S.	1939
分離脳		
カシオッポ, J. T.	Cacioppo, John T.	1951
社会的認知神経科学		
ガスリー, E. R.	Guthrie, Edwin R.	1886
学習, 連合, 刺激と反応の時間空間的接近理論		
ガットマン, L.	Guttman, Louis	1916
態度測定, ガットマンの尺度分析法		
ガードナー, H. E.	Gardner, Howard E.	1943
多重知能理論		
カナー, L.	Kanner, Leo	1894
自閉症		
カニッツァ, G.	Kanizsa, Gaetano	1913
ゲシュタルト心理学, 主観的輪郭		
カーネマン, D.	Kahneman, Daniel	1934
意思決定, プロスペクト理論, 行動経済学		
ガル, F. J.	Gall, Franz J.	1757
骨相学		
ガルバーニ, L.	Galvani, Luigi	1737
生理学者, 電気活動による神経伝達		
ガレノス	Galenus	129
脳室機能局在説, 精神の気		
カンデル, E. R.	Kandel, Eric R.	1929
神経生理学, 神経系の情報伝達		
ギブソン, E. J.	Gibson, Eleanor J.	1910
奥行き知覚, 視覚的断崖		
ギブソン, J. J.	Gibson, James J.	1904
生態学的知覚, 生態光学, アフォーダンス		
キャッテル, J. M.	Cattell, James M.	1860
反応時間, 個人差		
キャッテル, R. B.	Cattell, Raymond B.	1905
特性論, 16特性因子別性格検査, 知能		

キャノン, W. B.	Cannon, Walter B.	1871
生理学者, ホメオスタシス, キャノン=バード説		
キャンベル, D. T.	Campbell, Donald T.	1916
準実験計画, 内的/外的妥当性		
ギルフォード, J. P.	Guilford, Joy P.	1897
精神測定法, 知能の構造模型, 性格検査		
クライン, M.	Klein, Melanie	1882
新フロイト派, 対象関係論		
クレーク, F. I. M.	Craik, Fergus I. M.	1935
記憶の処理水準モデル		
クレッチマー, E.	Kretschmer, Ernst	1888
精神病理学, 類型論, 体型説		
クレペリン, E.	Kraepelin, Emil	1856
近代精神医学の父, 精神作業検査法		
クロンバック, L. J.	Cronbach, Lee J.	1916
信頼性理論, α係数		
ケイガン, J.	Kagan, Jerome	1929
発達心理学, 気質		
ゲゼル, A. L.	Gesell, Arnold. L.	1880
双生児統制法, 成熟優位説		
ケーラー, W.	Köhler, Wolfgang	1887
ゲシュタルト, 洞察, 移調		
ケリー, G. A.	Kelly, George A.	1905
パーソナル・コンストラクト理論		
ケリー, H. H.	Kelley, Harold H.	1921
原因帰属の分散分析モデル		
コスリン, S. M.	Kosslyn, Stephen M.	1948
心的回転, 心的イメージ走査実験		
ゴダード, H. H.	Goddard, Henry H.	1866
優生学, 犯罪, 知能, 遺伝		
コノルスキ, J.	Konorski, Jerzy	1903
神経生理学, 生理心理学, 条件反射		

コフカ, K.	Koffka, Kurt	1886
『ゲシュタルト心理学の原理』		
コリンズ, A. M.	Collins, Allan M.	1937
意味記憶, ネットワーク・モデル, 人工知能		
ゴルジ, C.	Golgi, Camillo	1843
ゴルジ染色		
ゴールトン, F.	Galton, Francis	1822
遺伝研究, 優生学, 相関, 共感覚		
コールバーグ, L.	Kohlberg, Lawrence	1927
道徳性発達理論		
ゴールマン, D. J.	Goleman, Daniel J.	1946
情動知能		
ザイアンス, R. B.	Zajonc, Robert B.	1923
単純接触効果, 社会的促進		
サイモン, H. A.	Simon, Herbert A.	1916
意思決定理論, 人工知能		
サーストン, L. L.	Thurstone, Louis L.	1887
比較判断の法則, 知能の多因子説		
サピア, E.	Sapir, Edward	1884
サピア=ウォーフの仮説, 言語相対性仮説		
サリヴァン, H. S.	Sullivan, Harry S.	1892
新フロイト派, 対人関係論, 関与しながらの観察		
シェパード, R. N.	Shepard, Roger N.	1929
心的回転		
ジェームズ, W.	James, William	1842
機能主義, 意識の流れ, ジェームズ=ランゲ説		
シェリフ, M.	Sherif, Muzafer	1906
同調行動, 集団規範		
シェリントン, C. S.	Sherrington, Charles S.	1857
神経生理学, 反射学, 感覚生理学		
シェルドン, W. H.	Sheldon, William H.	1898
胚葉に基づく類型論, 体型説		

シフリン, R. M. 記憶の二重貯蔵モデル, 短期記憶, 長期記憶	Shiffrin, Richard M.	1942
シャクター, S. 情動二要因説, 不安, 親和仮説	Schachter, Stanley	1922
ジャニス, I. L. 集団思考	Janis, Irving L.	1918
ジャネ, P. M. F. 神経症, ヒステリー症状	Janet, Pierre M. F.	1859
シャノン, C. E. 情報理論	Shannon, Claude E.	1916
シュプランガー, E. 価値志向に基づく類型論	Spranger, Eduard	1882
シュロスバーグ, H. H. 感情の円環モデル	Schlosberg, Harold H.	1904
ジョンソン-レアード, P. N. 認知心理学, メンタルモデル	Johnson-Laird, Philip N.	1936
ジンバルドー, P. G. 没個性化, スタンフォード監獄実験	Zimbardo, Philip G.	1933
スキナー, B. F. 徹底的行動主義, 行動分析学, オペラント条件づけ	Skinner, Burrhus F.	1904
スクワイア, L. R. 宣言的記憶	Squire, Larry R.	1941
スターン, L. W. 知能指数, 輻輳説	Stern, Louis W.	1871
スタンバーグ, R. J. 知能の三部理論	Sternberg, Robert J.	1949
スタンバーグ, S. スタンバーグ記憶走査課題, 加算要因法	Sternberg, Saul	1933
スティーヴンス, S. S. 尺度水準, べき法則	Stevens, Stanley S.	1906
スパーリング, G. 感覚記憶, 画像記憶, アイコニックメモリー	Sperling, George	1934

スピアマン, C. E. 　知能の二因子説，順位相関係数	Spearman, Charles E.	1863
スピッツ, R. A. 　ホスピタリズム	Spitz, René A.	1887
スピルバーガー, C. D. 　状態−特性不安尺度	Spielberger, Charles D.	1927
スペリー, R. W. 　分離脳，大脳半球の機能差	Sperry, Roger W.	1913
スペンサー, H. 　社会進化論，適者生存	Spencer, Herbert	1820
スペンス, K. W. 　誘因動機づけ，移調の行動主義的分析	Spence, Kenneth W.	1907
スポルディング, D. A. 　刷り込み，子の刻印づけ	Spalding, Douglas A.	1841
セリエ, H. 　ストレス，汎適応症候群	Selye, Hans	1907
セリグマン, M. E. P. 　学習性無力感，ポジティブ心理学，オプティミズム研究	Seligman, Martin E. P.	1942
ソクラテス 　古代哲学，無知の知，ソクラテス式問答法	Socrates	B.C.469
ソコロフ, E. N. 　定位反射，馴化	Sokolov, Evgeny, N.	1920
ソシュール, F. 　近代言語学の父，記号論の基礎	Saussure, Ferdinand de	1857
ソーンダイク, E. L. 　効果の法則，問題箱実験，教育心理学	Thorndike, Edward L.	1874
ダーウィン, C. R. 　進化論，『種の起源』	Darwin, Charles R.	1809
ダッドソン, J. D. 　覚醒水準，ヤーキーズ=ダッドソンの法則	Dodson, John D.	1879
ターマン, L. M. 　知能検査，ギフテッド研究	Terman, Lewis M.	1877

タルヴィング, E. エピソード記憶, 意味記憶, 符号化特性原理	Tulving, Endel	1927
チャルディーニ, R. B. 社会的影響, 説得のテクニック	Cialdini, Robert B.	1945
チョムスキー, N. 変形生成文法, 言語獲得装置	Chomsky, Noam	1928
ティチェナー, E. B. 構成心理学, 内観による意識内容の分析	Titchener, Edward B.	1867
ティンバーゲン, N. 動物行動学, 解発刺激, 4つの「なぜ」	Tinbergen, Nikolaas	1907
デカルト, R. 方法的懐疑, 心身二元論, 反射	Descartes René	1596
デシ, E. L. 内発の動機づけ, 認知的評価理論	Deci, Edward L.	1942
デューイ, J. プラグマティズム, 機能主義	Dewey, John	1859
トヴァスキー, A. 意思決定, プロスペクト理論, 認知バイアス	Tversky, Amos	1937
ドーキンス, R. 利己的な遺伝子	Dawkins, Richard	1941
トムキンス, S. S. 生得的基本情動, 感情の顔面フィードバック説	Tomkins, Silvan S.	1911
トリーズマン, A. M. 特徴統合理論, 視覚探索	Treisman, Anne M.	1935
トリプレット, N. 社会的促進	Triplett, Norman	1861
トールマン, E. C. 目的的行動主義, 認知地図, 潜在学習	Tolman, Edward C.	1886
ドンダース, F. C. 減算法	Donders, Franciscus C.	1818
ナイサー, U. 認知心理学	Neisser, Ulric	1928

ニューウェル, A.	Newell, Allen	1927
人工知能		
ニューカム, T. M.	Newcomb, Theodore M.	1903
社会規範, 態度		
ノーマン, D. A.	Norman, Donald A.	1935
情報処理心理学, インターフェース, ユーザビリティ		
ハイダー, F.	Heider, Fritz	1896
社会心理学, 帰属, 態度のバランス理論		
バウワー, G. H.	Bower, Gordon H.	1932
気分一致効果, 感情ネットワーク理論		
バークリー, G.	Berkeley, George	1685
英国経験論哲学, 連合心理学の先駆		
バドリー, A. D.	Baddeley, Alan D.	1934
ワーキングメモリー, 作動記憶		
バートレット, F. C.	Bartlett, Frederic C.	1886
日常記憶, 思考心理学		
パブロフ, I. P.	Pavlov, Ivan P.	1849
古典的条件づけ, 条件反射		
ハル, C. L.	Hull, Clark L.	1884
習慣強度と動因, 『行動の原理』		
パールズ, F. S.	Perls, Frederick S.	1893
ゲシュタルト療法		
ハーロー, H. F.	Harlow, Harry F.	1905
代理母実験, 学習セット		
バーン, D. E.	Byrne, Donn E.	1931
対人魅力		
バーン, E.	Berne, Eric	1910
交流分析		
バンデューラ, A.	Bandura, Albert	1925
社会的学習理論, モデリング		
ピアジェ, J.	Piaget, Jean	1896
認知発達段階, 発生的認識論, 知能・道徳性の発達		

ビアーズ, C. W. 精神衛生,『わが魂に出会うまで』	Beers, Clifford W.	1876
ピアソン, K. 生物測定学, 積率相関係数	Pearson, Karl	1857
ヒギンズ, T. E. 自己不一致理論	Higgins, Tory E.	1946
ビネー, A. 知能研究, ビネー式知能検査	Binet, Alfred	1857
ヒポクラテス 医学の祖, 四体液説	Hippocrates	B.C.460
ヒューベル, D. H. 視覚神経生理学, 大脳皮質における感覚情報処理	Hubel, David H.	1926
ヒューム, D. 英国経験論, 連合心理学の先駆, 人間は「知覚の束」	Hume, David	1711
ピリシン, Z. W. 視覚的注意, 多物体追跡, 心的イメージ	Pylyshyn, Zenon W.	1937
ヒルガード, E. R. 学習, 条件づけ, 催眠, ペイン・コントロール	Hilgard, Ernest R.	1904
フィッシャー, R. A. 実験計画, 統計, F検定	Fisher, Ronald A.	1890
フェスティンガー, L. 認知的不協和, 社会的比較過程	Festinger, Leon	1919
フェヒナー, G. T. 精神物理学, フェヒナーの法則	Fechner, Gustav T.	1801
プラトン イデア論, 心身二元論	Plato	B.C.427
フランクル, V. E. 実存分析, ロゴテラピー,『夜と霧』	Frankl, Viktor E.	1905
ブランズウィック, E. 知覚, レンズ・モデル	Brunswik, Egon	1903
ブリッジマン, P. W. 物理学者, 科学哲学, 操作的定義	Bridgman, Percy W.	1882

和名	英名	生年
プルチック, R. 感情の環, 感情立体モデル	Plutchik, Robert	1927
ブルーナー, J. S. ニュールック心理学, 認知発達	Bruner, Jerome S.	1915
プレマック, D. 心の理論	Premack, David	1925
ブレンターノ, F. 作用心理学	Brentano, Franz	1838
フロイト, A. 新フロイト派, 児童臨床, 自我心理学	Freud, Anna	1895
フロイト, S. 精神分析学, エディプス・コンプレックス	Freud, Sigmund	1856
ブローカ, P. ブローカ野, 運動性言語中枢	Broca, Paul	1824
ブロードベント, D. E. 情報処理過程, 注意のフィルターモデル, 意思決定	Broadbent, Donald E.	1926
フロム, E. 新フロイト派, 『自由からの逃走』	Fromm, Erich	1900
ペイビオ, A. U. 二重符号化仮説, イメージ・アナログ説	Paivio, Allan U.	1925
ベケシー, G. von 内耳蝸牛の研究, 聴覚細胞の周波数対応	Békésy, Georg von	1899
ベック, A. T. うつ病の認知療法	Beck, Aaron T.	1921
ヘッブ, D. O. 細胞集成体, ヘブ則, 感覚遮断	Hebb, Donald O.	1904
ベム, D. J. 超感覚的知覚, 自己知覚理論	Bem, Daryl J.	1938
ヘリング, H. E. 感覚生理学, 色覚の反対色説, 空間知覚説	Hering, Heinrich E.	1834
ベルガー, H. 脳波の記録, アルファ波の発見	Berger, Hans	1873

ヘルムホルツ, H. L. F. von	Helmholtz, Hermann L. F. von	1821
ヤング＝ヘルムホルツの三色説，聴覚の共鳴説，神経刺激伝導の測定		
ペンフィールド, W. G.	Penfield, Wilder G.	1891
ペンフィールドの脳地図，脳の機能局在		
ボウルビィ, J.	Bowlby, John	1907
愛着理論，マターナル・デプリベーション理論		
ポズナー, M. I.	Posner, Michael I.	1936
先行手がかり法，注意のスポットライト説		
ホーナイ, K.	Horney, Karen	1885
新フロイト派，社会文化的精神分析学		
ホームズ, T. H.	Holmes, Thomas H.	1918
ストレス，社会的再適応評定尺度		
ボーリング, E. G.	Boring, Edwin G.	1886
実験心理学史，感覚知覚研究		
ホール, G. S.	Hall, Granville S.	1844
米国心理学初代会長，米国初の心理学実験室		
ボールドウィン, J. M.	Baldwin, James M.	1861
こどもの進化論的発達，ボールドウィン効果		
ポルトマン, A.	Portmann, Adolf	1897
生理的早産		
マイケンバウム, D. H.	Meichenbaum, Donald H.	1940
認知行動療法，自己教示訓練，ストレス免疫訓練		
マウラー, O. H.	Mowrer, Orval H.	1907
学習の二要因理論，媒介過程説		
マグガイア, W. J.	McGuire, William J.	1925
説得への抵抗，接種理論		
マクリーン, P. D.	MacLean, Paul D.	1913
三位一体脳，反射脳，情動脳，理性脳		
マクレランド, D. C.	McClelland, David C.	1917
達成動機，コンピテンス		
マクレランド, J. L.	McClelland, James L.	1948
ニューラルネットワーク，並列分散処理モデル		

マズロー, A. H. 欲求階層説, 人間性心理学	Maslow, Abraham H.	1908
マレー, H. A. 社会的動機, 主題統覚検査	Murray, Henry A.	1893
ミード, G. H. 自己論, 主我と客我	Mead, George H.	1863
ミュンスターバーグ, H. 応用心理学, 精神工学	Münsterberg, Hugo	1863
ミラー, G. A. 短期記憶, マジカルナンバー7	Miller, George A.	1920
ミラー, N. E. 回避行動, 模倣行動, バイオフィードバック	Miller, Neal E.	1909
ミル, J. S. 心的化学, 『自由論』, 『功利論』	Mill, John S.	1806
ミルグラム, S. 権威への服従, スモール・ワールド現象	Milgram, Stanley	1933
ミンスキー, M. L. 人工知能, パーセプトロン, 『心の社会』	Minsky, Marvin L.	1927
メルザック, R. 痛みのゲートコントロール理論, 幻肢痛	Melzack, Ronald	1929
モーガン, L. 比較心理学, モーガンの公準	Morgan, Lloyd	1852
モレノ, J. L. ソシオメトリー	Moreno, Jacob L.	1892
ヤーキーズ, R. M. ヤーキーズ=ダッドソンの法則, 霊長類研究, 集団式知能検査	Yerkes, Robert M.	1876
ヤング, T. ヤング=ヘルムホルツの三色説, 光の波動説, 光の干渉現象	Young, Thomas	1773
ユング, C. G. 分析心理学, 集合的無意識, 内向・外向	Jung, Carl G.	1875
ラーエ, R. H. ストレス, 社会的再適応評定尺度	Rahe, Richard H.	1936

ラカン, J. M. É. 新フロイト派，構造主義，鏡像段階	Lacan, Jacques M. É.	1901
ラザルス, R. S. 認知的評価理論，ストレス・コーピング理論	Lazarus, Richard S.	1922
ラシュレー, K. S. 実験神経心理学，等能性の原理，量作用の原理	Lashley, Karl S.	1890
ラタネ, B. 社会的手抜き	Latané, Bibb	1937
ラッセル, J. A. 感情の二次元円環モデル	Russell, James A.	1947
ラメルハート, D. E. ニューラルネットワーク，並列分散処理	Rumelhart, David E.	1942
ラモン-イ-カハール, S. ニューロン説	Ramón y Cajal, Santiago	1852
ランゲ, C. G. 情動理論，ジェームズ=ランゲ説	Lange, Carl G.	1834
リッカート, R. 態度測定，リッカート法	Likert, Rensis	1903
ルビン, E. J. 図と地，ルビンの壺	Rubin, Edgar J.	1886
ルリア, A. R. 力動的局在論，神経心理学的検査，戦時脳損傷研究，失語症	Luria, Alexander R.	1902
レヴィン, K. Z. 場の理論，集団力学，アクションリサーチ	Lewin, Kurt Z.	1890
レスコーラ, R. A. 古典的条件づけ，レスコーラ=ワグナー・モデル	Rescorla, Robert A.	1940
ロジャーズ, C. R. 来談者中心療法，非指示的カウンセリング，エンカウンター・グループ	Rogers, Carl R.	1902
ローゼンタール, R. ピグマリオン効果	Rosenthal, Robert	1933
ローゼンツワイク, M. R. 環境と大脳皮質の発達	Rosenzweig, Mark R.	1922

和名	英名	年
ローゼンハン, D. L. 　精神疾患診断の実験	Rosenhan, David L.	1929
ローゼンブラット, F. 　パーセプトロン	Rosenblatt, Frank	1928
ロック, J. 　英国経験論, タブラ・ラサ	Locke, John	1632
ロックハート, R. S. 　記憶の処理水準モデル	Lockhart, Robert S.	1939
ロッシュ, E. H. 　プロトタイプ理論, カテゴリ認知	Rosch, Eleanor H.	1938
ロッター, J. B. 　統制の所在, 原因帰属	Rotter, Julian B.	1916
ローブ, J. 　刺激相称, 動物の相性研究	Loeb, Jacques	1859
ロフタス, E. F. 　目撃証言, 虚偽記憶	Loftus, Elizabeth F.	1944
ロマネス, G. J. 　逸話法による動物心理研究	Romanes, George J.	1848
ロールシャッハ, H. 　ロールシャッハ・テスト, 投映法	Rorschach, Hermann	1884
ローレンツ, K. Z. 　動物行動学, 刻印づけ, 刷り込み	Lorenz, Konrad Z.	1903
ワイナー, B. 　成功と失敗の原因帰属	Weiner, Bernard	1935
ワグナー, A. R. 　レスコーラ＝ワグナー・モデル	Wagner, Alan R.	1934
ワトソン, J. B. 　行動主義宣言, アルバート坊やの実験	Watson, John B.	1878

執筆者紹介 (50音順)

大対 香奈子 博士(心理学)
- 所属　近畿大学総合社会学部准教授
- 専門　応用行動分析学,臨床心理学,教育心理学

鈴木 まや 博士(心理学)
- 所属　関西学院大学,神戸女学院大学非常勤講師
- 専門　知覚心理学,感情心理学

中島 定彦 博士(心理学)
- 所属　関西学院大学文学部教授
- 専門　学習心理学,動物心理学,行動分析学

中道 希容 修士(心理学)
- 所属　関西学院大学,近畿大学非常勤講師
- 専門　学習心理学,思考心理学

成田 健一 文学修士
- 所属　関西学院大学文学部教授
- 専門　生涯発達心理学,老年心理学

藤田 昌也 博士(心理学)
- 所属　みどりトータルヘルス研究所,関西学院大学非常勤講師
- 専門　応用行動分析学,臨床心理学

堀川 雅美 修士(心理学)
- 所属　関西学院大学,兵庫医科大学,関西医療大学非常勤講師
- 専門　生理心理学,スポーツ心理学

安田 傑 博士(教育心理学)
- 所属　大阪大谷大学准教授
- 専門　パーソナリティ心理学,心理検査

Ⓒ 心理学用語研究会　2014

2014 年 4 月 17 日	初 版 発 行
2024 年 10 月 18 日	初版第 6 刷発行

英⇔和
心理学用語集

編　者　心理学用語研究会
発行者　山本　格

発 行 所　株式会社　培 風 館

東京都千代田区九段南 4-3-12・郵便番号 102-8260
電　話(03)3262-5256(代表)・振　替 00140-7-44725

港北メディアサービス・牧 製本

PRINTED IN JAPAN

ISBN 978-4-563-05233-1 C3011